DATE			

Intaglio
Simultaneous
Color Printmaking

Published by
State University of New York Press, Albany

For information, address State University of New York Press,
State University Plaza, Albany, N.Y., 12246
Design by Sushila Blackman
Typeset by Carolina Type, Durham, N.C.
Photography on part title pages by Jose Pelaez; courtesy New York University

Library of Congress Cataloging in Publication Data
Reddy, Krishna, 1925-
    Intaglio simultaneous color printmaking: significance of materials and
processes / N. Krishna Reddy.
    p.   cm.
    Bibliography: p.
    Includes index.
    ISBN 0-88706-739-5.   ISBN 0-88706-740-9 (pbk.)
    1. Color prints--Technique.   I. Title
NE1858.R43 1988
765--dc19

10 9 8 7 6 5 4 3 2 1

Intaglio
Simultaneous
Color Printmaking

SIGNIFICANCE OF MATERIALS AND PROCESSES

BY N. KRISHNA REDDY

Fremont - Newark
LEARNING RESOURCES CENTER
Community College District

"In the hands of the artist-printmaker, the intaglio plate, the materials, and the techniques form a web of dynamic, continuous patterns in which the artist is an active participant. In this way, printmaking becomes a living art—a path of learning and discovery through which to express oneself."

This book is dedicated to S. W. Hayter, printer and teacher.

Acknowledgments

In my pursuit to give shape to this book, I came upon friendly and genuinely interested students, artists and friends in whose company I developed these discussions. With their tireless cooperation, I gathered the needed material to enrich each essay in the book. I should like to express my deepest gratitude to them. I especially wanted to single out my students who have contributed to my work and generously helped me at every stage of the book: Susan Fateh, Martha Korduba, Jan Petersen, Marianne Sollosy, Andrea Zinn. In particular, my warm thanks go to Eric Edelman who aided me greatly in the preparation of the manuscript, and Prof. Paul Owen, Gerry Katzban and Michel Smith who helped me with the illustrations.

I would like to thank David Ecker, Director of Doctoral Program, Department of Art and Art Education, New York University; Gabor Peterdi, former Professor, Yale University; Una Johnson, Curator Emeritus, The Brooklyn Museum; Janet Siskind, Professor of Anthropology, Rutgers University; Percival Goodman, Professor Emeritus, Columbia University; Dale McConathy, Chairman, Department of Art and Art Education, New York University, for reading and commenting on the manuscript and for their generous advice; and I thank especially the late Stanley William Hayter, Founder-Director of Atelier 17, Paris, who guided me towards a more meaningful effort at every stage of the book.

Grateful thanks are also extended to the many museums and galleries for granting me permission to reproduce prints in their collections. Most of the black and white prints are the works of my students and my sincere appreciation is extended to them for their cooperation.

I also wish to acknowledge the assistance of Luis R. Cancel, Director, The Bronx Museum of the Arts. The museum is establishing a collection of works on paper of artists from Africa, Asia and Latin America and organized a retrospective exhibition of my work in 1982. Mr. Cancel read and commented on the work in progress and arranged for the loan of an IBM PC by the Bronx Museum which facilitated the creation of the manuscript for this book.

I also gratefully acknowledge the kindness and cooperation of Dr. Rustum Roy, Director of Materials Research Lab at Penn State University, and Dr. Dennis Kunkel, Department Of Neurological Surgery, University of Washington, Seattle, two great scientists who freely gave invaluable help in providing me with microscopic photographs of an assortment of crystals and other materials.

Special thanks to William Eastman, Director of SUNY Press for his initiative, and to Carola Sautter, Acquisitions Editor with SUNY Press, and Sushila Blackman, Graphic Designer, for their deep involvement in helping to give this book its present form.

And finally, I wish to express my deep appreciation to my wife Judy Blum and to my daughter Apu, for their invaluable help and advice in the conversion of the manuscript to an actual book.

Contents

LIST OF ILLUSTRATIONS

COLOR

BLACK AND WHITE

Frontcover: "The Great Clown," by Krishna Reddy. Courtesy of Galerie Borjeson, Malmo.

Preface

Printmaking, like painting and sculpture, is a language—a language of forms, of lines, textures and reliefs—in which the artist expresses himself. It is one of the most inspiring means of expression, with its powerful graphic gestures and essential simplicity. The wealth of materials and processes, and their wide range of effects, make printmaking unique in the field of art. As new images inspire the artist to discover fresh ways and means for expressing them, the field is in a constant state of renewal, full of experiment and innovation. It is of paramount importance for the artist to explore the materials and get closer to them, rather than attempt to master them as an aloof technician.

The processes involved in working a plate and making a print from it are pathways of learning and discovery. Recognition that the image is shaped by a material process brings clarity, humility, and a sense of participation in the act of composition to the artist. The closer one gets to the materials—the more one learns of their nature, their behavior and their interaction—the more pliable they become to one's senses. One works directly and spontaneously—like a potter feeling for his image through the clay. This journey into the deeper sources of materials should heighten our sensibilities and deepen our understanding, essential in creating a vital work of art.

This intimate feeling for material processes can be experienced as we look through the prints of Rembrandt, Goya, Blake and Picasso. They solved their pictorial problems working intimately with the graphic materials in miniature dimensions. Rembrandt, with only an etching needle, obtained incredible pictorial effects—velvety darks against shimmering lights—with cross-hatchings. Goya realized his intensely vital images with an extraordinary use of aquatints. Blake made his conceptions visible through powerful relief etchings. Picasso sharpened his sensibilities through becoming deeply involved in the plate; his contributions were enormous. It is unfortunate that today, in an increasingly complex atmosphere of growing technology, we are beginning to lose this original sense of the medium.

The technique of printmaking has evolved rapidly over the past forty years. It has become a major medium of the arts, taught in universities and art schools and practiced everywhere. There are some five thousand workshops around the world today. Workshops like Hayter's Atelier 17 in Paris and Rolf Nesch's in Oslo, where international artists gathered to work and experiment, have become well known. During the Second World War, European artists visiting the U.S. set off intense printmaking activity. In the forties, Hayter's Atelier moved to New York and pioneered American printmaking, bringing together adventurous and committed artists whose experiments inspired others. Since that period advances in printmaking have been made in the U.S..

As more and more artists took to the medium, printmaking grew rapidly; as a result, an endless variety of new techniques and materials emerged. Working in an atmosphere of fast-developing technologies, artists created increasingly complex works. These works lent themselves to an obsession with technical invention for its own sake. The sudden popularity of prints, coupled with existing competitive, commercial pressure, generated an emphasis on the making of a print as a product and its reproduction. Printmaking, as an original art form, rapidly deteriorated into a process of reproduction. To practice printmaking under today's circumstances requires a long apprenticeship and a host of materials and equipment. The expertise and competency required to work in this area have become distractions for the artist, turning him into a technician and master-printer.

For these reasons, inspite of great technological advances, printmaking is undergoing a profound crisis. The working artist finds himself far distanced from the creative potential of the medium. If he becomes preoccupied with product-oriented mechanical ways, he loses touch with the soul and spirit of the medium. Therefore a careful discussion is needed at this time on the nature of materials and processes of this potent medium. This discussion is the focus of this book.

The idea for this book came to me nearly ten years ago when I created a special workshop called "Color Print Atelier" at New York University, which was designed for a select group of practicing artists, teachers and special students. The workshop task of presenting the latest and most advanced techniques of "Viscosity Color Printmaking" opened up new avenues to my teaching.

It became clear to me that the real issue was how to structure the course so as to bring the complex materials in printmaking closer to the artist in order to achieve simplicity and directness, qualities essential to building an image in a spontaneous and meaningful way. Instead of presenting the students with ready-made recipes or formulas as solutions for their work, I encouraged them to take journeys on their own—to learn through their own investigations and discover their own need for initiative and freedom.

In this atmosphere of international artists and teachers, discussions became central to our meetings—discussions exploring the meaning of materials and instruments and the evolution of printmaking. These sessions were times of great revelation and learning.

This book is in part the result of these workshops and meetings. Primarily, it grew from my studio notes over the thirty-five years of work in the field. These notes record

1. Master B. G. ''St. Anthony and St. Paul.'' XV Century. Burin engraving.
Collection, The Metropolitan Museum of Art, N. Y.

my deep involvement with the experiments I carried out, especially in the new areas of viscosity color printmaking, which later led to a number of discoveries and technical breakthroughs. Today these processes are practiced in nearly every workshop devoted to intaglio printmaking. And finally, this book has grown from the knowledge I gathered through my teaching work at Atelier 17 in Paris, at New York University, and as well through seminars and workshops I have given as a visiting artist in universities and art schools all over the world.

Besides discussing materials and processes in printmaking to reach a deeper comprehension of them, this book centers on the new areas of viscosity color printmaking from intaglio plates. To my knowledge there has been no comprehensive manual on these subjects.

The new developments in intaglio printing created new possibilities for existing processes. The process of applying both intaglio and surface colors simultaneously by various methods to the intaglio plate has added new depths and dimensions to the print. This new way of printmaking is a highly integrated and powerful process—full of experiment and innovation; it includes all the techniques of printmaking, such as litho, relief, serigraphy, and so on. In turn its influence is felt in all other areas of printmaking.

The discussions that follow on new ways of simultaneous structuring of intaglio and surface colors include—in addition to offset, stencil, contact, etc., the techniques developed at Atelier 17—all the new developments in contemporary intaglio printmaking since the 1930s. Special chapters are devoted to the latest and most advanced areas of color printmaking by viscosity methods. One chapter, ''Color Printmaking in the Pointillist Manner,'' is on a newly developed process to print colors in dots or broken streaks. This is a highly simplified method—as simple as black and white intaglio. All these processes are sufficiently detailed in this book so as to provide a practical manual for both students and working artist-printmakers.

New ways of working the plate, besides etching and photo-processes, involve conceiving and working on the plate with sculptural methods—carving and engraving it directly with hand and machine tools. With the new methods of preparing the plate and selectively depositing both intaglio and surface colors simultaneously on the same plate and printing it in one operation, we have achieved a color print of great graphic quality, with a directness and immediacy never before realized.

The latest innovation of printing in pointillist or broken colors, when fully developed and perfected, will bring about a tremendous change in intaglio color printmaking. It will simplify technical processes while creating powerful and intense color fields. This area of printmaking is developing into a complete and most expressive process—full of innovation and experimentation.

My visit to Hayter's Atelier 17 in Paris in 1951 was an eye-opening experience. Soon after World War II, artists had gathered there from many countries looking for a new freedom. They were seeking to bring this feeling into their work and into their lives. Coming from a country that was just emerging from nearly a thousand years of occupation, I

2. Rembrandt. "Girl With Hair Falling On Her Shoulders." 1635.
Line etching, first state. Collection, The Metropolitan Museum of Art, N. Y.

found such a free atmosphere a revelation. The Atelier was a place of great activity and experiment. Artists worked together, pooling their discoveries and achievements.

In pursuit of direct expression, these artists sought to integrate and simplify the many elements in printmaking. Their passion was for color and they tried integrating it into the intaglio print. When color was joined to it, intaglio printmaking grew in complexity. They found the existing traditional methods of printing color from multiple plates too mechanical and too indirect to work a print, although perhaps convenient for predictable reproductions. Artists at the Atelier looked for more direct ways. Experimenting by trial and error, they began to discover various ways to superimpose a number of colors simultaneously on a single intaglio plate—offset, contact, stencil processes, to mention only a few.

As a working sculptor, I began to regard the intaglio plate as a piece of sculpture. In the free atmosphere of the Atelier, I was on my own and could take my own journeys. I wanted to rediscover existing printmaking materials and techniques, and understand them. Through the process of building an image I watched it evolve. I was also curious to

3. Pablo Picasso. ''Vigil.''1936. Combination etching.
Collection, Museum of Modern Art, N. Y.

4. Francisco Goya. "A casa di Dientes" (Hunting for Teeth) from *The Caprices*. 1792.
Etching and aquatint, second state. Collection, The Metropolitan Museum of Art, N. Y.

learn about the formation of a fish, an insect or a man in nature. Pondering the shape of a fish in movement, I began to see its form as a dynamic expression of the total environment; I could visualize it as a whirlpool spinning out of a web of interpenetrating and radiating movements.

Trying to explore this concept in the process of building an image which should take shape in terms of materials, tools and machines, I saw it had gone through a total transformation. It fascinated me to watch how each new image, in trying to realize itself, set me into motion—inspiring me to find new ways and means to build it. All of these feelings could have been inherent extensions of myself at that period; but ever since that time, when I started searching into materials and processes, I have been unable to see or think as I had before.

I have reminisced here about my involvement in the Atelier environment merely to prepare the ground for a discussion of these new processes at length. In the course of this book, I also venture on excursions into areas of thought that might deepen our sense of materials. I am convinced that perceiving the significance of materials is essential to our understanding, and to the possibility of bringing out the meaning and beauty of our concepts.

Significance
of Materials
& Processes

P A R T   O N E

1 Processes as Experiment and Exploration

Sowing a seed is only one part of a process. Watch how all the elements of nature got to work, spurring the seed. Mark the splendor of its radiating roots, branches, leaves and flowers that themselves carry seeds in innumerable numbers. As the seeds are ejected they in turn radiate again and again, continuously repeating the cycle. We can visualize the unceasing reverberations of these dynamic patterns go forth in space time. It is as if we throw a pebble in a pond and watch the extraordinary ripples that it sets off. It is as if we touched the very fabric of the universe—the pulse of nature, its essential process, one of movement and continual change.

The seed, in the process of becoming a tree, is not an isolated entity adrift in flowing time; it is engaged in a dynamic and complex interplay with the environment. We understand the visible phenomenon, the formation of the tree, as part of the whole rhythmic pattern that permeates the process of nature. We are exhilarated by being in tune with the ceaselessly moving reality. It is as if our minds were lost in music, extraordinarily quiet, deeply silent, responding to incoming sounds. Music is a continuous process in time, sound and space. By our act of sowing the seed, we placed ourselves within the movement of nature's rhythm. We experience true joy in responding to the excitement, wonder and mystery of the continuous dynamic processes of reality.

This way of looking at reality raises our sense of participation and leads us to discover our abilities in all fields of endeavor. Man's mind is vast and all-encompassing. It is endowed with refined sensitivities and senses. When freed of as many encumbrances as possible, it can embrace the unceasing motion and continual change that is reality.

In one of life's paradoxes, we are driven to find a place of tranquility and refuge from this endlessly changing "chaotic" nature, over which we have no control and which we cannot comprehend. But for what reason? We human beings, because of the uncertainty of life and fear of death, may have contrived our internal world—a world of highly organized fragments of memory and thought systems—a collection of words, images, symbols, knowledge, ideas and beliefs. We express ourselves in terms of these crystallized agencies and units. The meaning of perceived objects and our reactions to them is to be found in their relation to one another. They connect and interact so well to produce our present consciousness or intellect.

This internal world of ours is not an indifferent ensemble but an active, participating force, with an ability to think abstractly and symbolically, allowing a wealth of perceptions and memories, reasoned thoughts and actions. It is orderly, regulated and compartmentalized. Its internal program, or concept, can quantify the world and make its own physical-spatial interpretations, with a certain depth of creative imagination.

It is our mind that we see reflected in every manifestation of nature. And we have managed to create a world on our own image. It is interesting to examine the subjective side of our conditioning, both in our creations and observations—the way we feel, think and perceive. We begin to see that all our fabrications are produced by the texture of our overlapping consciousness and thought systems. In our participation with our environment, it is interesting to watch the way we respond to and construct knowledge by actually incorporating perceptions into certain memory patterns. We see the way we perceive or construct objects, as presuppositions of our own organism, in terms of elementary components: basic geometrical forms and shapes, the primary colors, tones, lines and linear measures.

We see the outside world in simple geometrical abstractions in the midst of the confusing variety of shapes in nature—a tree might look like a combination of a cylinder and a cone or a sphere. Another example is the way we prune garden plants into regular shapes. This vision is also reflected in things we design and build—how we apply basic geometrical shapes to a table, a house, a skyscraper, a factory, a city and in fact everything we have covered the earth with. Even the most intricate aspects of physical shapes are factored to these simple geometrical abstractions. Watch the way we have created our world of paradoxically great beauty in terms of basic colors and tones emerging from our own limits. Observe our ways of reaching the outer world in linear measures—the way we frame space. The subjective character of our interpretations is well expressed in the artist's work. Impressionists, Cubists and Surrealists revealed this subjectivity with clarity and understanding.

This fascinating universe within us—the intellect—is capable of creation and beauty. Magnificent and reliable as our mental concepts are, however, they cannot adequately probe the recesses of reality. Actually, this artificial interior of ours creates enough inertia to prevent us from truly living. This humanly conceived system, with its building blocks—mechanistic models and symbols—forms a stable and predictable order that we can rely upon. But by reducing nature to some measurable scale of values, we have succeeded in creating an objectified world, separate from us.

In its preoccupation with frozen thought systems, our intellect has no place for such things as love, compassion, beauty, wonder, life—as these are not measurable or analysable. Intellect does not allow for the deeper emotions and feelings that cause the true human intelligence to function.

With the clamor and never-ending movement of its thought, our intellect keeps us from an intimate participation in the world. Conditioned to this narrowness and distorted living, which we have allowed ourselves, we seem to be more or less adjusted to our world. This we call living and to this we cling. In this state we have become separated and we live reduced as strangers to our bodies and minds. Caught up in ourselves we become petty and limited and self-serving. Once we wake up from this torpor and learn how we have distanced ourselves from our true being, we shall recover our freedom. We will start to live a meaningful life.

However much our intellect distorts our lives and our perceptions, we do not give up our innate curiosity, imagination, creative intelligence and our urge to experience reality. We are an exploratory species. As we strive towards a deeper understanding of this phenomenon (that is our mind) we learn more about ourselves. And this inquiry reveals freedom. In freedom we regain our astounding capacity for creative intelligence and understanding, and draw on our deeper resources. One must be free to look. If the mind cannot be free it will close in on itself and deteriorate.

In the world of nature nothing stands still. Nature is in a state of constant movement and change. As a part of it, and embedded in it, the human being forms an organic whole with nature. Through the understanding that our reality is the background from which we emerge, we get closer to reality by participating in it. As part of living reality, which is essentially a dynamic process, our life is movement. As it constantly confronts the new and the unknown, our life can function in wholeness—as we gather all our senses, emotions, intellect, our whole being and act as one.

A mind that can change becomes timeless, selfless, and overflowing with creative power; and it has the vitality and energy needed to plunge into the depths of reality and unravel it. It is a mind immersed in the process of everchanging reality, engaged and exploring. By placing itself in the flow with reality, it is in a deep state of learning.

Attached to our rememberances, beliefs, habits and dogmas, we have built and anchored an image about ourselves. In order to sustain this image we struggle, to become. To fulfill and deny being. And as our brain is programmed to drive toward a particular goal, it cannot respond to or participate in the process of living. In escaping from the present we have become insensitive to our moment-to-moment existence.

Since we have to achieve, we desire to control fully the new object, fearing its dynamism and flux. In similar fashion, out of weakness, an artist making a picture puts himself on center stage. He struggles to master the various materials and processes in his drive toward achievement. He has stopped playing with materials. But play is infinitely important as it is the very heart of creativity.

An artist who has stopped playing denies his own being. An artist who cannot change and be fluid in his ideas is not really alive. In the hands of an artist-printmaker, the intaglio plate takes on tremendous significance. He discovers, in the interaction of the plate and other materials, a web of dynamic patterns with himself as an active participant in the process.

By getting closer to the wealth of materials, becoming involved in the plate and the color print, and gaining insight into their nature, the artist discovers that each material represents an infinite continuum of possibilities and together they are interactions in patterns of activity. This awareness sets the artist in motion, allowing him to participate in the dynamic processes of both materials and the emerging image. There is learning and excitement—dialogue and discovery—in this moment-to-moment involvement. Experimentation and exploration contribute to the awakening of his deeper sources.

With exhilaration we watch a conductor and an orchestra raise a piece of music to great heights. In his total involvement, his closeness to every instrument and the artist-creator behind it, and his sense of participation with the entire orchestra, the conductor brings out great feeling in the music. In this atmosphere it is not any single individual but the process generated by the ensemble that triumphs.

2 Life of Materials

In pondering and learning the meaning of matter, we see new vistas through which to deepen our experience. A speck of dust may appear as dirt to a solely practical person. But to a contemplative mind the dust speck is a revelation—it throbs with life. It is an unfathomable entity.

These are the feelings of a mind that is close to reality—that looks at Nature's being and its invisible mysteries.

By taking this approach to materials, we are not indulging in a flight of fancy; rather we are attempting to experience the world afresh, at another level, with innocence, truth and love. To a person who looks only at the physical and utilitarian value of things it may sound insane to consider these things alive with unearthly beauty. Yet this pitifully limited view has become the normal human condition.

Particles of matter are "of nature." Knowledge of how these particles interact with each other makes it easier to grasp the function of organic nature as a whole. By being committed and involved we begin to understand the dynamic properties of all forms of matter. Endowed, as we are, with a mind, refined senses and an appetite for learning, we can explore the innermost recesses of matter to learn its true nature.

A sense of personal exploration is essential to the practicing artist—to learn the material, to comprehend matter and its meaning. In the process of this journey the artist comes closer to materials, sharpens his sensibilities and deepens his knowledge.

As an artist gets increasingly involved with materials he becomes aware of their infinite variety; each one continuously flows into the other without boundaries. Materials are a vast range of possibilities, not a limited collection of objects. Accordingly, as he participates more and more with materials, the artist searches for unity in their endless variety. In a developing image he senses formation and transformation of matter. Materials then become more pliable and meaningful in expressing his state of mind through the image.

As the artist's concepts, ideas and ideologies take over, everything else (including materials) passes him by. He uses the surface of a canvas or a plate to work out his ideas, without knowing much about his material. More aggressive artists want to master materials, thereby ignoring their inherent qualities. But the true artist, in his more caring effort, draws upon the inner nature of the materials.

We possess a mind with innate curiosity, which, through acute senses and an ability to imagine, is prepared to meet this marvelous world. We have an urge to touch and handle matter, to probe it. At this point we experience a deep sense of connectedness with our own surroundings. We belong to our environment and are sustained and nurtured in it, like an embryo in the womb.

However, in our isolated, man-made world of today we have created barriers to this complete union. Within our social environment we have allowed ourselves to be reduced to less than what we truly are, with less and less opportunity to live actively or creatively or even think critically about our behavior. As a result of years of conditioning we have become habituated to this way of life and are unable to live up to our potential.

To understand this condition we have only to witness the spectacle of a child descending to this earth, radiating life force. As he descends he is grabbed and readily stamped and marked with a name; and all of society goes to work on him, systematically hammering and molding him until he fits the peculiar course that we consider "normal." In the long, steady process of ideological indoctrination through family, school, church—indeed the whole of society—the new human being is estranged from himself and humanity. In this state of constant interference he becomes a stranger to himself, stripped of most of his innate qualities. His passionate inner life has been erased.

We are all such traumatized people, more or less adjusted to a confused world. Living in our present environment has limited our capacity to think. Our capacity even to see, hear, touch, taste and smell is shrouded in veils of our own fabrication—our prejudices, our assumptions and superstitious beliefs. These obstruct our sense of reality.

It is strange to watch how we human beings, in a state of reduced awareness, preoccupied with our psychological security, try to separate ourselves from the presence of ceaselessly changing reality. Seeking shelter, we board up the windows and doors of our sense openings, encircling ourselves with layer upon layer of rigid and ready-made concepts. We live in the suffocating interior of our pretensions. In this state of narrowness and distortion, we have become reduced and self-indulgent, and insensitive to the outer world.

Take for example, the way we have labelled everything around us with names and symbols. We have surrounded ourselves on all sides with a wall made of labels, replacing actual things with the symbols we have created. These endless names and symbols clog our minds and hinder clear thinking and perception. We stop short at the outward appearance of natural things and content ourselves with the labels and concepts we have pinned onto these indescribable phenomena.

We give the name "Flower" to a natural phenomenon and store it in memory, as we do in a computer. The computer registers the name we insert, but it has no idea of the phenomenon. Likewise, our intellect has become a collection of memories and thoughts derived from the mechanistic symbols we have created. Intellectually we have no way of knowing what reality is. To face living reality we have to transcend everything that conceals from us the true being of things. It is important for us to recognize this limitation—the words and symbols we use to wrap up living things.

Responding to the excitement of a flower, we say in a hurry it is "beautiful," even before we can experience it afresh. What we call "beautiful" is a product of our thought or imagery—a projection or extension of ourselves or the texture of our inherent nature. In reality the flower is neither beautiful nor ugly. It is a phenomenon in itself, a living organism to be explored. It is beyond naming. To set aside the name we gave the flower, to wander anew into its world, is to go through an extraordinary experience. With great wonder we find ourselves in the midst of meaning, learning and discovery. We have within us a deep urge to learn of the fascinating life of materials.

How we view, how we experience, how we conceive of the mystery of life in our minds deserves deep study and contemplation. Upon questioning deeply, we become aware that we create things in our own image in the presence of over-protective thought systems. We need to explore and break through the narrow circle of our mechanistic concepts, symbols, memory and thoughts which interfere with the act of perception. We need to realize how our inner psychological activity seems always to dominate the outer reality. We need to see how our ideals, prejudices, beliefs and faiths limit our capacity to think and understand.

This perspective helps us to investigate the very nature of our existence and the different facets of our fragmented and alienated thinking. We understand how we are separated from reality by the walls we have created. We have to transcend human conditioning by eliminating all that lies between us and reality, in order to come face to face with reality. The feelings and sensitivities we develop, in the process of exploring and learning the life of materials, open up fresh possibilities for our own actions and our relationships with mankind and our environment.

3 State of Mind and the Environment

We stand between the immense cosmos and the unfathomable universe within us. If we pause for a moment and watch these great mysteries, we are filled with awe and wonder. There is an urge in us to discover and learn what lies behind these mysteries, the hidden reality that is the very source of life. Just as our bodies want nourishment, our minds want to know. This urge to learn and understand is in almost everyone.

As children we are overwhelmed by our surroundings. We marvel at everything that our senses bring to us. And as we mature, we begin to learn by looking more intensely at nature. We have a constant longing to escape from the surface of things and travel beneath to discover what is happening below that surface. Inquiring and questioning, we learn and understand, as reality unfolds layer by layer.

A healthy mind that is fully open, free from prejudices and narrow attachments, develops an ability to see things as they really are—to see things in their wholeness. When the mind enters into this state of learning there is creativity; there is the opportunity to be truly alive moment-to-moment. This form of learning is the most effective way to develop a more profound vision, to develop our full potential as human beings.

Preoccupied with self-centered activities, worried and anxious, driven by insecurity, we are unable to meet the reality outside ourselves. Self enveloped, we become insensitive to everything. Introvertedness denies intelligence; self-centered activity and active learning pull in opposite directions.

The human mind is nature's greatest resource. It is intelligence and heart combined, and it is capable of deep vision. It is essentially creative. We have not yet had the time to explore this extraordinary resource. We must strive to build a better environment for life on earth, where we can grow in total freedom, and fully express ourselves.

Despite such infinite human resources, we are witnessing a world where humanity, as a whole, has slowly drifted away from the flowing river of living reality, and built for itself a material environment based on mechanistic concepts and thought systems. We live in a world of frozen memories and ideas and have little contact with reality.

To have a secure world and to have firm hold on life, man has created things in his own image. He has covered the earth with cities and civilizations of his own making. He has propagated, spreading like a new growth, over the entire surface of this planet. He himself lives surrounded by narrow walls, made up of the names and symbols that he has given to things. He views the world in terms of this thinking; it has little to do with real life.

Instead of intimately participating in the world of nature, man has placed trust in efficiency and organization and became involved in rearranging the world. He has built a network of socio-political organizations, only to be faced with endless wars and destruction. Man has divided himself into groups based on race, religion and nation, and clouded himself with ignorance and prejudices. Buried deep under the multiple layers of man-made organizations, he is unable to get disentangled from the distortions thus created.

The ''Developed Western World'' has built an industrial society in which speed and specialization in every field serve to isolate human beings. There, despite visible prosperity and order, man stands in degredation, totally alienated from himself and the rest of humanity.

The mercantile organization, which is based on money and power, has systematically cultivated human vices such as greed and envy; through its ideology of efficiency and organization, it has carved out a world of its own. This commercial world is destroying the natural world. Commercial culture has spread into every realm of human existence, even infiltrating human feelings.

Living in an ambitious and competitive environment, and trying to survive, human beings have become self-enveloped and corrupt. To feed our fantasies, we set goals, and in trying to attain these goals we get programmed by them. In our drive for achievement, we become aggressive and ruthless, forgetting our capacity for great insight and generosity. The more we are preoccupied with ourselves, the closer we are pushed toward a complete break with our true being. In our present environment, we have allowed ourselves to be reduced to less than what we are.

As we watch the entire surface of this planet being changed through our actions, it is important that we discuss these concerns. We have struggled and surrendered our lives to build this extraordinary world of ours, only to find ourselves in deep conflict with our own being and with each other. As the world becomes a more unfriendly place, polluted physically and spiritually, we begin to realize the consequences of our shallow actions. It is strange that we, who are so sophisticated in certain fields, are yet so unresponsive to the true reality of human life. The recognition that we have to function in

19

wholeness and find for ourselves the meaning of life, will ultimately lead to a change in the course of our actions and to a recovery of our total freedom.

The real crisis is not so much in the outside world as it is within ourselves—in our minds, hearts and our actions. We should take the initiative to observe, to understand our own being and the world surrounding us in all their complexity. It seems apparent that the true course of our happiness lies along this path—the path of learning about our true selves, about our relationship to one another and to the spiritual and material world.

If we are to survive without deteriorating into meaningless mechanical life forms we have to recognize the need for a new vision of the living world. We have to recognize a fundamental change in our thinking and our actions. We have yet to create a civilization or a social framework where we can live with full use of our creative potential. There is a great need for a more profound understanding of this world, through deeper learning and wider education.

This earth, so subtle and enduring, is an unimaginable marvel. We recognize ourselves only as a part of this living organism. We are of it as we are embedded in it. As we become aware that we ourselves are manifestations of nature and not isolated entities, we begin to feel our deep connection to it. In this feeling we discover wonder and delight in all manifestations of life on this planet. We realize there is no limit to our capacity to exist in the soul and spirit of this planet. As our understanding of the life processes of the earth's organism grows in intensity, our existence in it gains a deeper significance.

New Ways of Simultaneous Intaglio & Surface Color Printmaking

PART TWO

4 Introduction to Simultaneous Structuring of Intaglio and Surface Colors in Printmaking

The delight of printmaking comes through the search for a means of expressing one's ideas. The processes involved in working a plate and making a print from it are full of learning and discovery. It is of fundamental importance to explore the techniques and materials we use in making a print, as it is these materials that participate in the process of building the image.

The complexity of techniques and materials in printmaking can lend themselves to an obsessive development of technical invention for its own sake. The pressure from the social environment is for a type of commercial manipulation that directly opposes creative experimentation. Techniques are presented to us as proven formulas to be followed. If we follow the dictates of a formula we lose the initiative essential to building a meaningful image. If we do not question the techniques, they become our authorities.

An artist, preoccupied with survival or his drive to succeed, uses the materials to make a successful commodity. He cannot allow himself the time or pleasure to find his own questions to ask or problems to solve; he makes a product but not an expressive image. He approaches the materials in a greedy and conventional way without any regard for them; thus a distance is created.

The question the artist asks must be a real one, a question of his own even if others have asked similar ones. It may have been asked before and the artist may find a new solution or the solution that others have found before him. He may be guided by a teacher or find the answer in antiquity or invent a brand-new technique, but if the question is real, the answer—the completed image—will be real as well, and therefore, expressive, satisfying and meaningful. Involvement is the key: involvement in a question—about the world, about color, about people, about space—and involvement in the materials—plates, tools, acids, aquatints, inks.

The artist's attempt to evolve his concept by working with the materials, rather than merely elaborating on existing techniques, can yield a breakthrough to simplification—such as the leap from using several separate plates in the process of color printing to the simplicity of simultaneous color printing using a single plate. This simplicity may then be elaborated so that another plate may be added or the single plate printed twice. In the same way, the superimposition of colors by viscosity processes leads us to the simplicity of pointillist and broken-color structuring (techniques that are later explored here). With a deeper comprehension of all these materials and techniques and their integration, we can achieve a fuller and richer means of expression. Each breakthrough adds not just a new technique to be mastered but an integration of experience with materials and expression. The technique itself may appear at first to be the transcending factor, such as the use of viscosity in printing, but it is the deeper understanding of the relationship between inks and how this relationship may be directed to meet the artist's aims that is the real breakthrough. Through the various stages of elaboration and simplification, the artist must strive to see and express the image clearly.

Trying to explore the development of the image which must take shape in terms of materials, tools and equipment, we find the image that has been produced in the process has been totally transformed. The deeper our understanding of everything that participates in our expression of the image, the more dynamic and powerful the image becomes. This experience, gained by a mind open to experiment and free from fixed ideas and formulas, cannot be replaced by intellectual substitutes or through knowledge acquired from books.

Pondering the fish swimming in the stream, we become aware of the fish formation as a dynamic expression of the environment. In the same way, the image forms as the dynamic expression of its environment—the interactions of all the materials, tools, processes and the artist. As a part of this environment, the artist will naturally feel the growth of sensitivity, curiosity and the deep involvement in the process of building the image.

In simultaneous intaglio and surface color printmaking we use a variety of materials. Besides the plate there are the acids to etch the plate, the tools (both hand and machine) to work with, the inks for printing, different rollers to superimpose inks in the plate, and so on. Each of these behaves differently in the printing process; so it is of the utmost importance for us to have a deeper understanding of all these materials—their basic structure including their physical and chemical natures—and, most of all, their interaction. The more sensitive and closer we are to the materials, the more pliable they become to our state of mind, adding to the spontaneity and creative intensity of our work.

24   The discussion of printmaking that follows includes a description of many tradi-

tional materials and techniques which are still useful. Each may contain potentials yet to be explored. The main focus of the discussion, however, will be the new ways of simultaneous intaglio and surface color printmaking. These new methods enable us to simplify and integrate the printing process. We can work directly on the plate, carving the image with hand and machine tools as in sculpture. With the new methods of selectively depositing both the intaglio and surface colors on the same plate we can print all the colors in one operation. In this way we can achieve a color print of great graphic quality and with a directness never realizable before.

5 A Brief History of Color Printmaking

Its Beginnings

In history printmaking started as a medium of communication. The initial function of the print was to make information visual. Stamps and seals made in ancient America, Egypt, China and India are thought to be the first prints. Prior to the invention of paper, the print was used as applied decoration on textiles. Printmaking proliferated in Europe towards the end of the fourteenth century when paper became available there.

The earliest attempts in color printing were hand-colored stencils and wood blocks. In the illustrations of fifteenth century publications, they depicted passages from the Bible. Prints served as icons for the common man, souvenirs of shrines, New Year's cards, playing cards and illustrated popular ballads.

From the fifteenth through the seventeenth centuries, goldsmiths and metal chasers used engravings to decorate metal plates, armor, candlesticks, jewelry and articles of precious metal. One of these fifteenth century metalsmiths must have taken a print from an inked metal design; the earliest prints on paper survive from this time. These prints are basically ornamental in form.

Albrecht Durer, originally trained as an apprentice goldsmith, engraved metal plates and took prints on paper. He engraved with lines the forms of his images and suggested the three-dimensional solidity with cross-hatching, to convey an impression of light and shade. Like Durer, William Blake was another example of a trained craftsman who was able to transcend the limits of his craft to fashion a new way of artistic expression. In the course of his life he evolved from a commercial reproductive engraver to an inspired, innovative and prolific graphic artist. His line engravings conveyed his original images in a simple and straightforward manner. He actually composed his images directly on the copper plate, giving his engravings an added vitality.

Driven to create new images by his visions and dreams, and fueled by his sensitivity to materials in the printmaking process, Blake slowly revealed the sculptural qualities inherent in his plates. He remains, in his time, an isolated instance of originality—in his development of new ways of printmaking and his regard for the plate as sculpture. Blake experimented also with infinite varieties of color printing. He opened up new possibilities for graphic experimentation.

In the seventeenth century, artists discovered etching to be a more flexible process than engraving. It eventually replaced engraving as a more popular creative medium. Artists started using the needle as a pen, and experimented with acid to bite the lines further. Rembrandt's use of pure etched line is an outstanding example. He experimented with various patterns of etched lines and close cross-hatchings, and to heighten the effects of light, shade and varieties of tone, he used dry point.

During the mid-eighteenth century, J.B. Le Prince pioneered the first consistent use of aquatint. Goya, however, is the greatest exponent of aquatint. He is the artist-printmaker who made the most effective use of aquatint's tonal qualities.

Technical innovations in black and white printmaking continued to evolve in the eighteenth and nineteenth centuries. With each new development of the black and white plate, artists sought an analogous adaptation using colors.

In Pursuit of Color

The pursuit of color in printmaking resulted in a new level of complexity in both processes and materials. One of the earliest attempts was to print a plate in two or three neutral tones, the chief coloring being added by hand directly on the prints. These impressions cannot in a strict sense be called color prints. They might be called colored prints. This way of making the print is the antithesis of a true printer's method, but it leaves the artist a perfectly free hand. The infinite variations possible make it essentially an artist's process. The finest examples are the colored etchings of Hercules Seghers (1589–1635). His attempts to find a new means of imbuing his prints with color led to a unique and expressive technique: first he colored the paper or linen by hand; he then printed the design of the etched plate on the material, and with color, touched up the design by hand. His rugged, etched line was achieved by a method similar to contemporary lift ground.

William Blake's experiments advanced color printmaking considerably and anticipated modern processes. Being an artist outside convention, he was free to develop some extraordinary methods of etching in relief. Finding no publishers for his unusual and unpredictable work, he took to producing editions himself.

Blake made a colored print by first printing the plate in one color (he used yellow, blue and green as well as black for intaglio) and then tinting the printed design by hand

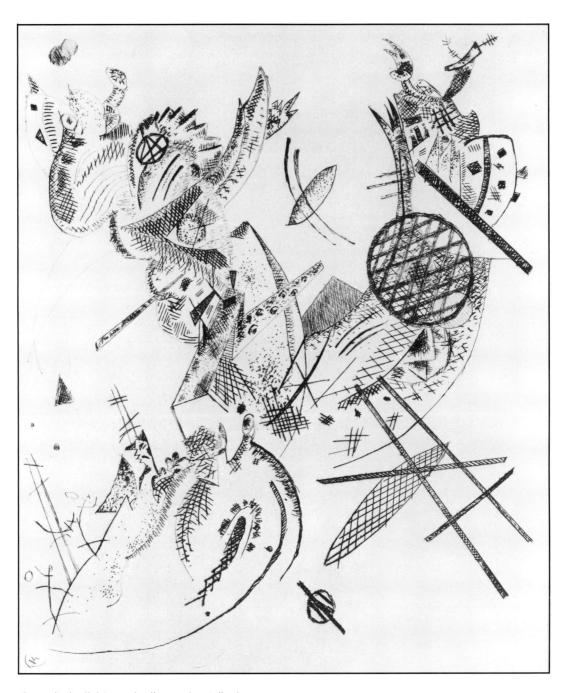

5. Wassily Kandinsky. "Kleine Welten". Drypoint. Collection,
The Metropolitan Museum of Art, N. Y.

in watercolor. To strengthen his design he would then often apply rich opaque colors to the prints. He found a transfer method for applying heavy tempera colors to the print: first he would paint a card in tempera in the full color range of his design; then he would transfer that color to the plate by rubbing the card against it. His prints showing highly-textured opaque coloring must have resulted from such a method. The heavier mottled surfaces in these prints might have resulted from dusting dry colors over the surface of the wet impression. His experiments yielded a small number of impressions filled with variations.

During the seventeenth century, a handful of artists started exploring new means of integrating color with prints—in what might be called *color-prints*. They produced the first color print from etched and engraved plates. Artists such as Frederick Blomaert (from the Netherlands) used the ''chiaroscuro'' method of getting surface color; that is, using several wood-blocks in combination with engraved and etched plates.

Breaking away from both the classic subject matter and the technique of the chiaroscurists, Johannes Teyler's (1648–1697) experiments led to multicolor inkings of one etched or engraved plate. He was able to use as many as six colors to create a painterly

6. Paul Klee. ''Two Nudes''. 1907.
Zincograph. Collection,
Museum of Modern Art, N. Y.

effect. In this process, rag stumps ("dollies" or "poupées") were used to ink the plate. This was a lengthy procedure, as delicate divisions of color were required. The colors were in the lines or mezzotinted areas. Other etchers continued to work with this method, making plates with a combination of etching, line engraving, mezzotint and roulette work; they were inked "a la poupée" and printed. Some etchers tried using two separate plates, one a key plate and the other an aquatint—each part of the aquatint plate applied with a different color. But great care was needed in aligning the paper on each plate for its impression.

In the eighteenth century, the three-color process of color printing was developed from the theory of primary colors (that all colors are derived from the primary colors—blue, yellow and red). Jacob Le Blon (1667–1741) carried out impressive experiments in developing the three color printing process. He used three separate plates for the three colors and tried to combine them to give a true composite result. Often he used a fourth plate for his blacks. With the imperfect means at his disposal, he could not produce any satisfactory prints. The colors failed to combine in a predictable manner and sometimes turned muddy. But he continued to experiment. His basic idea is employed today in the most modern mechanical applications of color printing.

In the nineteenth century, engravers, etchers and mezzotinters tried various ways of color printing, using both intaglio and surface colors on the etching plates. Some of them used wood blocks for surface colors, in combination with their plates. George Baxter, an English printer, sometimes used as many as twenty blocks to realize his various tints. He applied this method for reproducing masterpieces of paintings. He made thousands of very successful color prints.

During the last half of the century we hear of such reproductive printers and of their subtlety with techniques. But printmakers who practiced the art of original etching were isolated. Some of the French landscape painters of this period revived original etching. Degas was among the first artists to experiment with monoprint; starting with monochrome prints, he advanced to prints in full color. Seurat, Bonnard and Toulouse-Lautrec used lithography to produce very powerful poster images. Artists during the latter part of the nineteenth century, influenced by existing aesthetic revolutions, pursued new means of expression. Many were attracted to the versatility of the color print.

Modern Printmaking

The development of color printmaking encompasses the struggles of many individuals with materials and techniques, in their attempt to print color images fully expressive of their ideas. At times, artists, impressed by the graphic qualities and richness of materials, experimented freely with them. They sought for simplicity in expression. Frequently there were master-printers (reproductive craftsmen) who looked for methods of predictably reproducing an image. Their contributions are considerable. The real history of printmaking, however, lies in the array of materials and processes that have been passed on from master to apprentice, from teacher to student, and from artist to artist. Each artist starts from where a past colleague left off and selects and combines different materials. His particular findings, small inventions or revolutionary perspective, become part of the potential for other artists of his time and the future.

This outlook may help us to understand the art of printmaking in our time.

The manipulation of color for its expressive value has been the overriding pursuit of color printmaking early in our century. The Post-World War I art movements which challenged the traditional boundaries of art proliferated in Europe; movements like the Rev-

7. Joseph Hecht. ''Gazelles''. 1949. Burin engraving. Private Collection.

olutionary School of Moscow and the later Dadaists introduced new forms of expression. In this tumultuous atmosphere printmaking workshops became meeting places for artists interested in printmaking and learning. Some artists like Hayter in Paris and Rolf Nesch in Oslo established workshops and invited others to join them. They imbued the workshops with the spirit of innovation. Later these studios flourished as international centers for younger artists.

Hayter established Atelier 17 in 1926 to develop print media as another means of expression and bring them closer to the artist. The Atelier's primary focus was on experimentation and the discovery of new technical and expressive possibilities in printmaking, particularly intaglio. Artists discovered the beauty of the plate, and found that the materials posed exciting technical challenges.

Hayter's adventurous spirit attracted artists from around the world. At that time many of the Surrealists, such as Masson, Max Ernst, Miro and Tanguy worked in the Atelier. Curiosity and learning were in the spirit of the place. They saw the value of color printmaking and tried ways of integrating it with the image. They found the prevalent color printmaking methods lacked the freedom and spontaneity they considered essential; such methods were too mechanical and distanced the artist from the material. The multi-plate process failed to satisfy artists for these reasons. They felt the need to bring colors together and superimpose them simultaneously on one plate, printing it in one operation.

The experiments artists carried out in simultaneous color printmaking during the twenties and thirties in the Atelier formed its philosophy and very foundation.

The struggle to pull colors together onto one plate continues at the Atelier to the present day. Artists have tried and developed various techniques of simultaneous color printing. They sometimes tried combining other techniques with an intaglio plate: printing on the plate together with litho, silkscreen, linoleum and wood block, etc. Artists such as Miro and Masson experimented with open biting portions of the plate for long periods of time, thereby creating deep crevices or sometimes eating away entire portions of the plate. They rolled the plate surfaces with colors (in the manner of wood blocks).

Artists at the Norwegian workshop of Rolf Nesch took another approach to color printmaking. They would solder bits of copper wire, washers and other "found objects" of metal to the plate or cut up pieces of other etching plates and join them in new positions by soldering; then they would emboss a sheet of printing paper with these built-up plates uninked or add rags and other small and flat objects dipped in color to them. Often they would apply color to the recesses and spaces in the plates and roll their surfaces with another color.

At the Atelier in Paris, artists experimented with ways of applying colors both in the intaglio and relief parts of the plate before printing it. Through trial and error they developed various ways of superimposing colors simultaneously on a single plate. Among some of the successful processes were:

Offsetting Colors. Offset printing the colors on the plate from various textures, collages, wood-cuts, lino-cuts, and so on.

Combination of Techniques. Printing litho, silkscreen, etc. together with an intaglio plate.

Rainbow Colors. Offsetting a film of colors in juxtaposed stripes onto the plate with intaglio.

Stenciling Colors. Superimposing a series of colors through stencils onto a plate.

Contact Process. Rolling various colors on a thick sheet of glass, putting the intaglio plate face down on each color and transferring them by pressing the back of the plate.

A later development in simultaneous color printmaking was the viscosity process, described later in Chapter 7 B.

The spirit of Atelier 17, as well as its existence, attracted artists and students from around the world. When the Atelier moved from Paris to New York during the Second World War, almost single-handedly it revitalized the American interest in printmaking.

Many Atelier students from around the world returned to their home countries to start printmaking workshops that embody the philosophy of Atelier 17—the spirit of openness to experiment and innovation, of sensitivity to materials and processes, and of comradery and growth that the working together of many minds and hands brings.

Printmaking Today

In 1940 Atelier 17 closed down in Paris; it was reorganized in the United States, starting as an intaglio class at the New School in New York. Many American artists, including Pollock, Lipchitz, Lasansky and Peterdi came to work there. These artists and many others, deeply devoted to printmaking, continued the Atelier's tradition of experimentation in the classes and workshops they taught. The influence of the Atelier has spread up to the present time; today, there are nearly 4,000 printmaking workshops in America—in university art departments, art schools, and as private workshops and art centers. Frequently, there are shows devoted exclusively to prints in museums and art centers in major American cities. The recognition by galleries and auction houses, publishers and collectors, of the value of prints did not lag far behind. Many printmakers' associations, print clubs and graphic publishers emerged in all parts of the country. Never has the financial backing for printmaking been so available nor the media of printmaking been so visible.

There has been exceptional public enthusiasm in America for printmaking—the energy and resources poured into this medium have been unparalleled in the rest of the world. The enthusiasm of artists for printmaking led them to search for new materials and techniques. This approach resulted in the elaboration of the print, since new materials and methods were piled one on top of the other in its execution.

One is led to wonder, however, whether these developments in printmaking have really affected the artist for the better. It is useful in this context to compare printmaking in Europe and America. The European art movements of the late nineteenth and early twentieth centuries regarded the medium of printmaking as having significance equal to that of painting and sculpture. The Post-Impressionists, the German Expressionists, the Fauves and the Suprematists needed to convey through art their concern with human values. These artists participated directly in the making of their own prints. They recognized the importance of printmaking as a personal medium.

Whereas in Europe printmaking was accorded equal status with painting and sculpture as a medium of expression—given its due as a way of life—in America printmaking does not seem to have taken root as a form of artistic expression in its own right.

It has remained a relatively minor medium. There have been admirable practitioners in the area who knew their medium thoroughly and understood its beauties, often hailed as masters. But there was not a strong printmaking movement in America to parallel the movements in painting and sculpture.

Famous American painters and sculptors used printmaking as a medium to reproduce their work. Edition publishers filled galleries and collections with prints. Such mass production required the services of many artists-turned-printers. In such an atmosphere, artist-printmakers who indulged in serious printmaking were encouraged to dabble in technology and create sensations through their inventions.

Education has been a prime cause of this situation. Young artists studying the graphic arts in school are urged to emphasize technique in their work rather than develop their initiative and curiosity. The system encourages them to emulate the passing fashions of the galleries. As a result the young printmakers have become product-oriented. They have lost the impetus to produce any meaningful work.

It is important for the artist, sitting down to work with the plate, to have an awareness of the history of the printmaking medium. We see how, over a period of five hundred years, the preoccupation with producing large numbers of prints has led to an emphasis on the reproducibility and predictability aspects of the printmaking process. The trend of reproducing oil paintings in color prints has allowed mechanical methods to dominate printmaking. We observe that product orientation results in a concern with the surface of the plate and its exploitation as the mere vehicle for a printer's ideas.

When a sensitive artist works in the medium, however, it takes a different turn. Rembrandt, Goya, Blake and others made tremendous changes in printmaking as an artist's medium, in their search for greater expression of their images. They realized the potential and richness of printmaking—how it integrated the qualities of both painting and sculpture, but transcended them in its deep involvement with materials.

The deeper the artist, the greater the vitality gained by the medium. In the hands of those with little to say—that is, with surface preoccupations—printmaking becomes restricted and mechanical.

The plate has emerged through all of these influences, positive and negative, as a most powerful medium; as a true artist's medium. It has developed added dimensions of immediacy and directness, both as a sculpture and as a rich synthesis of the colors that it imparts to the print.

6 Plate Preparation: Materials and Processes

Discussion

Traditionally, etching and engraving have been limited to a play of lines and tones, with the etching plate used merely as carrier upon whose surface the image was drawn. The other areas of printmaking—wood block, lithography and silk screen—have also shared this preoccupation with surface. The wood or linoleum block, the stone or planographic plate, and the screen have existed to gratify the artist's play of ideas. When the reproductive aspect of printmaking has dominated the field, stifling experiment and creativity, artists have worked with these materials without any deep regard for their true nature and behavior. And yet the approach to these media is close at hand in the intaglio plate, to be freely and openly explored.

First, let us place the metal center stage, and take note of some of its characteristics. Most of us are too quick, in any creative activity, to assume the dominant role—our voice, after all, clamors the loudest! But a more humble attitude brings with it the realization that there are many participants, each with a distinct contribution. Here we only learn through the sense of participation with the plate; our desire to dominate it will teach us nothing.

Due to imaginative experimentation, the versatility of etching and its rich potential as a means of expression are continuously being revealed. But perhaps most exciting of all is the realization that the plate has intrinsic sculptural qualities, that it lends itself to carving and sculpting—a far more intimate and sensitive approach than one that is merely mechanical and involves the use of gadgetry.

From this perspective, the concern is now as much with the depths, the interior of the plate, as with the surface composition. As a preliminary experiment, take a small etching plate and see how many times it can be placed in acid—each time creating a distinct level—before eventually biting through to the back: you will be presented with a very long flight of steps! The effect of acid on aquatint creates myriad, minute, indentations which may not appear particularly substantial to the naked eye, but it takes only a little imagination (or a magnifying glass) to see that one wanders amidst towering pillars, in a canyon of stalagmites. In effect, the plate has the capacity to become a landscape, full of hills, valleys, wide and narrow rivers, smooth or rocky plateau. And just as subtleties and changes in weather contribute to nature, so climate and atmosphere are given to this landscape by the use of inks, the choice of colors and the method of their application.

To prepare such a plate, a certain amount of relief is necessary, whether it be caused by open-biting, by aquatint (which is actually deep-bites in miniature) or by breaking up the surface of the plate with a variety of tools. The principle behind any of these techniques is the same: to create a range of depths within the plate which will in turn contribute to the density of the print, whether in black and white or in color.

Deep biting with acid produces stepped levels down into the plate, thus forming a succession of reliefs. The action of the acid creates hard edges, which will show up as heavy linear structures in the print. These may be kept as a bold, well-defined image, or they may be modified—by use of a scraper, emery paper and burnisher—revealing subtle, undulating structures.

Playing with halftones—worked by means of aquatint, photographic dot screens, or hand and machine tools—can bring extreme subtlety and richness to the print. Minute indentations in the plate create porous areas. When printed in the simultaneous color process, dots and streaks of pure color are juxtaposed side by side, producing effects similar to those sought after by the Impressionists. Seen from a distance, the print has an overall quality of richness, made up of shimmering areas of luminous color. The half-tone can be also scraped down to form shadows of the initial work, thus probing the illusory as well as the actual dimensionality of the plate.

One criticism constantly leveled against the intaglio color printmaking medium is its lack of directness; the fact that it shackles spontaneity. To some extent, this is true, if one works with grounds and with acids. However, with the use of tools, and particularly machine tools, the plate becomes an exceptionally pliable and receptive substance. The intimacy and directness with which the plate can be worked and shaped makes it akin to sculpture and painting.

The experience of handling tools, whether hand or machine, brings the artist in very close contact with the materials, and especially with the plate. Once a healthy awareness and sensitivity have been established, the plate is seen to be an extremely pliable substance. Developing images is now considered in terms of direct carving, engraving and gouging, with no recourse to acid. Hand tools, while they can be the most laborious method of working a metal plate, give the greatest sense of intimacy. However, machine tools enable the entire plate to be worked with such ease that image-building, or its removal, becomes rapid. Machine tools encourage spontaneity and can be of great value in strengthening the expression of the artist. Furthermore, the use of hand tools and machine tools is akin to the directness of contact experienced in painting and sculpture.

This extraordinary medium is capable of absorbing the principles of many other artistic areas—relief processes, painterly approaches, photographic depiction, to name but a few. Directly related to the immediacy of working the plate with tools is the simultaneous process of color printing, in which rollers of different densities interact with the varying depths of the plate. The wide range of roller densities available (from very hard to a soft gelatine surface) renders them extremely sensitive to the landscape of the plate.

A. Etching

Etching may be broadly described as the art of drawing and working a design into a metal plate with some acid or mordant; an impression or print is then taken from it. The deep reliefs, lines, textures, tones, etc. are obtained with the use of various acid resistant grounds, acids, tools, etc. The corroded or etched areas in the plate possess a positive value, and stand for the design itself. Printer's ink is applied to the plate by means of a dabber and wiped clean. A humid paper is placed against the plate and pulled through the intaglio press underneath layers of special blankets. (See Glossary).

The elements involved in etching are: etching ground, needle, acid and plate.

Ground is an acid-resistant substance used to cover and protect those parts of the plate that we do not want to be bitten by the acid. Most grounds contain three ingredients: rosin, asphaltum and beeswax. Rosin provides adhesive strength; asphaltum further strengthens the ground and increases its resistance; beeswax makes it pliable and flexible so that fine lines may be drawn in the ground without it flaking. By changing the relative proportions of these three ingredients one can change the properties of the ground. For example, line etch requires a ground that will not flake off when one draws a line; the ground must be flexible enough to allow fine lines to be drawn on it. To improve flexibility, one increases the proportion of beeswax. For deep bite reliefs, however, the ground should contain a greater amount of asphaltum, to resist acid concentration over a long period of exposure. Ground preparations are available in both solid and liquid forms. Liquid etching ground is made from a hard ground by dissolving it in Benzine or Varnoline, thereby making it easy to work directly on the plate.

The needle used to draw the design should be properly prepared. Its point should be blunt so as not to scratch the metal through the ground; this could cause foul bite. Needles of various thicknesses can be used to obtain a variety of line thickness. Even objects such as nails can be used for thicker lines.

The most common acid used in etching is nitric acid. It is carefully diluted with water to etch fine lines and used in more concentrated form to produce deep reliefs. If the acid is extremely strong it will underbite lines and reliefs, creating sharp edges and jagged textures. These can be very powerful and beautiful.

In judging the strength of the acid one should rely on sense rather than measurement. The behavior of the same solution of acid is different in different situations, so one should be sensitive to the particular conditions in etching the plate at hand. Only trial and error will show how to regulate the strength of the acid. Bubble formation indicates acid strength. When the acid is very concentrated the plate is covered with very active bubbles, which rise off the plate to the top of the acid bath. When the acid is not very strong one should make sure the surface of the plate is covered with bubbles; otherwise the acid is not working. In general the stronger the acid, the greater its bubble formation.

Nitric acid is very dangerous and one should learn to handle it carefully. It corrodes skin and clothing and gives off brown fumes which are dangerous to breathe.

1. Line Etching

Line etching is made by applying ground to a metal plate, then tracing or drawing image and dipping plate in acid bath.

Materials

A metal plate (copper, zinc or steel) with corners and edges beveled	*Scraper*
	Burnisher
Grounds: hard ground or liquid etching ground and liquid asphaltum	*Acids: Nitric Acid, Dutch Mordant or Iron Perchloride*
A variety of paint brushes	*Files*
Etching needle and other tools to mark through the ground	*Polishing materials: snake stone, charcoal, metal polish, kerosene, alcohol*

Procedure

- ☐ Coat the plate with hard ground using a flat, soft brush. Spread it evenly on the plate and allow it to dry thoroughly.
- ☐ Trace main compositional lines onto the ground by means of transfer paper or alternatively, draw directly with the etching needle.
- ☐ Trace or draw freely on the plate, but take care not to press the needle too hard and scratch the metal underneath the ground.

- Any mistakes at this stage are easily corrected by careful over-painting with liquid hard ground or stop-out varnish.
- Immerse the plate in a bath of nitric acid, of a strength usually no more than 8 parts water to 1 part nitric acid. (Set the acid bath under a hood or in a well-ventilated area.) An exposure of ten minutes to the acid will give a good quality of line to the plate. The longer the plate sits in the bath, the deeper the exposed lines will be bitten. By leaving some lines exposed and stopping out others by masking with hard ground, one can boldly emphasize the exposed lines with repeated acid biting.
- Remove the plate out of the acid. Rinse the plate, front and back, under cold, running water. Using a rag, clean it with a mixture of kerosene and alcohol. Let it dry and take a trial proof of it. A special intaglio printing press is used to pull these proofs. (See Glossary).
- To build rich tonal areas of light and shade, one can cross-hatch in a series of layers, biting each layer separately in the acid.
- If mistakes happen in etching the plate they can always be scraped and burnished down. Rough surfaces are polished with snake stone, charcoal and metal polish.

8. Grounds and oils used in etching

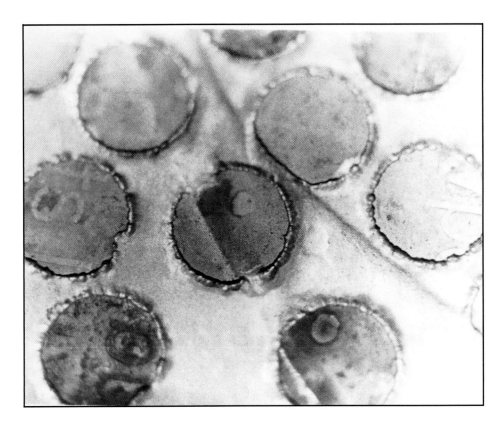

9. Bubble effect
in deep-etching

2. Soft-Ground Etching

Soft-ground is made by adding grease, Vaseline or tallow to hard-ground (and made into liquid soft-ground with Benzine or Varnoline). The resulting soft-ground mixture when applied to the plate remains soft and tacky, unlike hard-ground. Any textured material pressed into the soft-ground picks it up, exposing the bare metal in the pattern of the material. Soft-ground is used for the transfer of a wide variety of textures of man-made or natural objects pressed by hand or run with the plate through a press. Objects like cotton and nylon fabrics, crumpled and folded pieces of paper or aluminum foil, strings, leaves, feathers, can be used—these open up new possibilities for experimentation. Due to the transparent nature of many of the textures, especially the tightly knit fabrics, it is also possible to build up a series of overlays to give a range of tonal gradations.

Materials

A metal plate
*Soft-ground (liquid) and hard-ground
  (liquid)*
Nitric acid
Etching needle, scraper, burnisher, flat file

Paint brushes
*A variety of cotton and nylon fabrics and
  other materials such as paper, strings,
  leaves, feathers, etc.*

10. Preparing the plate by etching

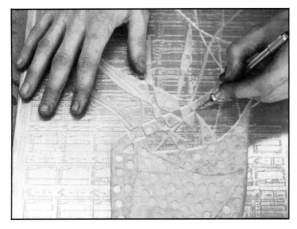

1. Cutting and peeling of contact paper for deep etching

2. Working aquatints in the plate by etching (magnified detail)

3. Working tones with a vibro tool

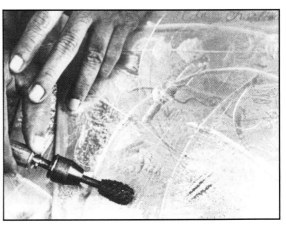

4. Working tones with a textured cutter

5. Gouging (magnified relief)

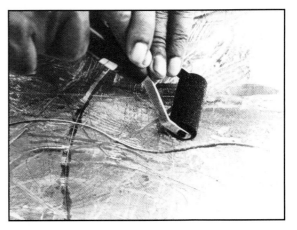

6. Working tones with a large roulette

11. Soft ground etching:
Experiment by Sara Weisman

Procedure

- Apply soft-ground to the plate with a wide,soft brush; after a while, press a flat object with a textured surface into it. When the object is lifted the soft-ground that touched it lifts off as well, leaving metal exposed in the pattern of the textured surface. Make desired changes with stop-out varnish or liquid hard-ground. Proceed to bite plate as in line etching (with a medium acid strength of 8 parts water to 1 part acid). A trial proof can be taken.
- If desired the plate can be re-covered with soft- ground, new textures pressed into it and rebitten.
- Textures can also be superimposed to achieve rich tonal gradations. Tightly-knit, sheer fabrics (such as nylon, silk or rayon) could be used in this process. One can etch these textures into the plate and bite the plate repeatedly, each time adding new textures on top of previous ones. (Areas that have reached a desired tonal quality can be protected during subsequent etching by covering them with stop-out varnish.)
- When running textures through the press, take care to cover the objects and the plate with a sheet of wax paper to prevent the blankets and press bed from being ruined by the squeezed-out ground.
- Undesirable textured areas can be removed by scraping them down with a scraper and burnishing them. Scraped areas may be polished with emery paper, charcoal and snake stone with water.

42

3. Halftone Process by Aquatint Method

Building with tones is the simplest and most powerful way to create an image. To achieve tonal gradations, we need to roughen the surface of the plate, making an ink-holding ground that creates the tones. There are many ways of doing this. The plate can be roughened with hand tools such as roulettes (which come in many textures) or a rocker with machine-powered cutting and grinding heads made of metal and stone, or by acid-etching porous grounds (including photo-etching, spray grounds and rosin grounds).

The classical tonal method—and the earliest—is a rosin ground aquatint: the etching of a plate covered with rosin dust. Inspite of its antiquity, aquatint is still practiced today. It is a process that every artist virtually reinvents for himself. Inspite of the length of time aquatint has been in use, it remains a beautiful new territory to explore. Aquatint is capable of tonal distinctions which no other method can produce. And it has an element of surprise.

It is important to understand in this process the action of the acid on a plate covered with fine grains of rosin. When the acid bites the plate it lowers the level of metal all around the grains; if the acid is not too strong, it leaves the metal directly underneath the grains standing up in the form of tiny pillars. As the plate passes through the press

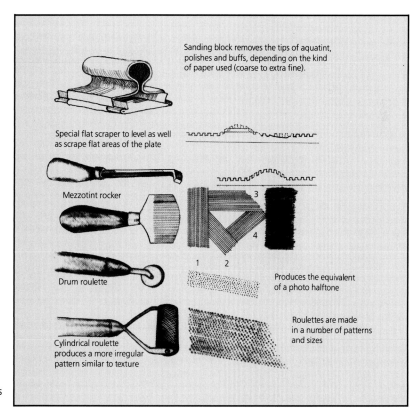

Sanding block removes the tips of aquatint, polishes and buffs, depending on the kind of paper used (coarse to extra fine).

Special flat scraper to level as well as scrape flat areas of the plate

Mezzotint rocker

3

4

1   2

Drum roulette

Produces the equivalent of a photo halftone

Cylindrical roulette produces a more irregular pattern similar to texture

Roulettes are made in a number of patterns and sizes

12. Diagram: Hand tools to build tonal effects

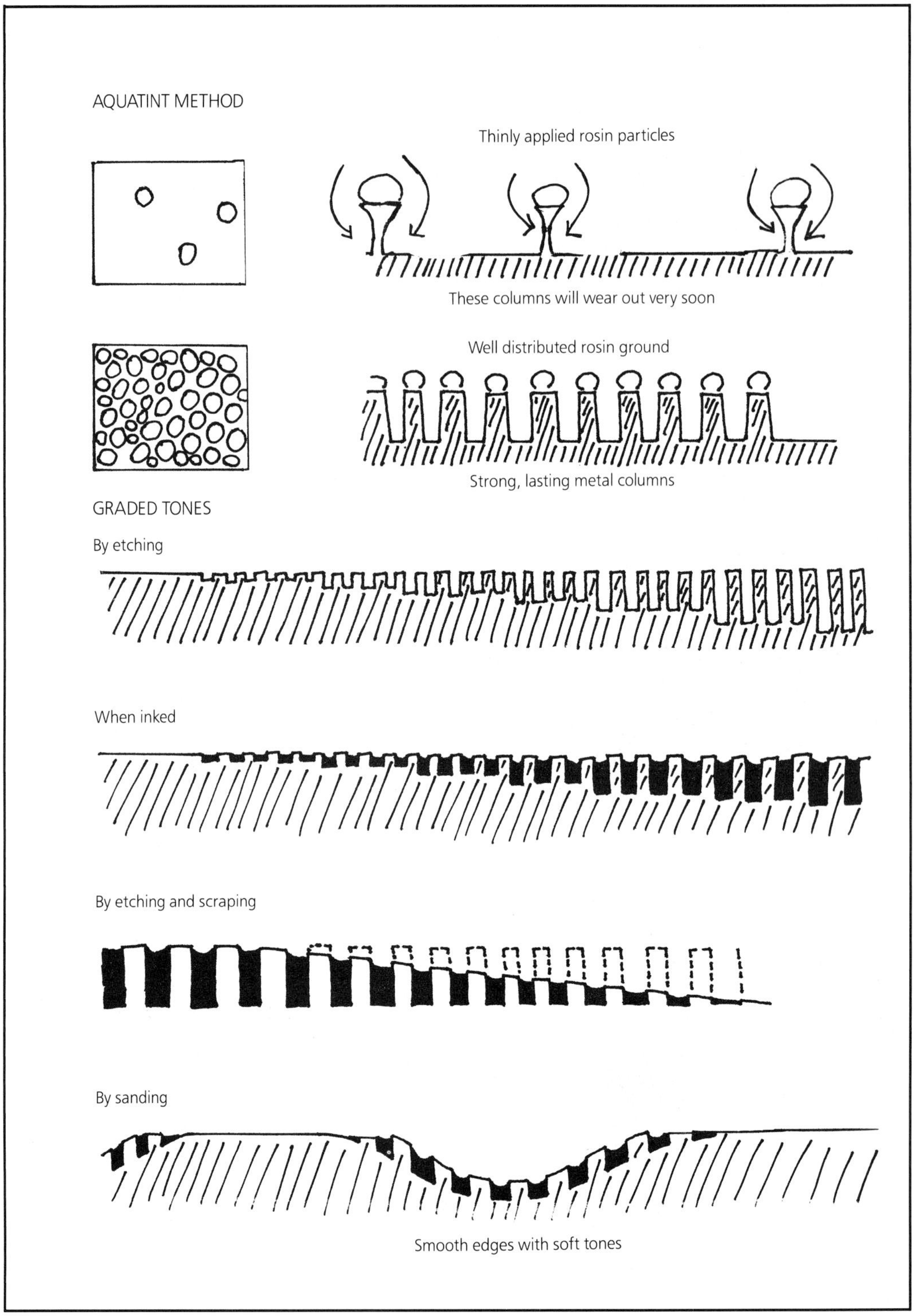

AQUATINT METHOD

Thinly applied rosin particles

These columns will wear out very soon

Well distributed rosin ground

Strong, lasting metal columns

GRADED TONES

By etching

When inked

By etching and scraping

By sanding

Smooth edges with soft tones

13. Diagram: Building half-tones and textures in the plate

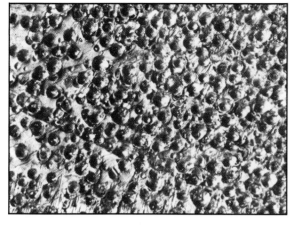

1. Worked with a vibro tool

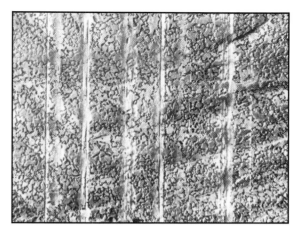

2. Textures from heavy aquatint

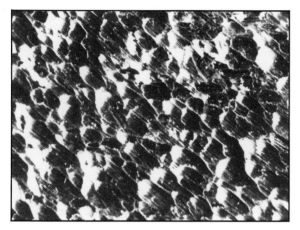

3. Worked with a textured head

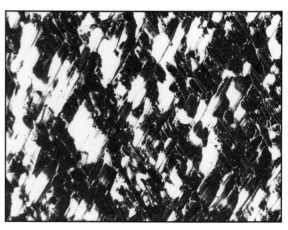

4. Worked with a serrated metal head

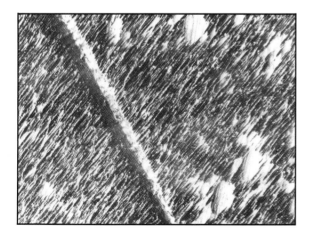

5. Worked with closely-serrated tool head

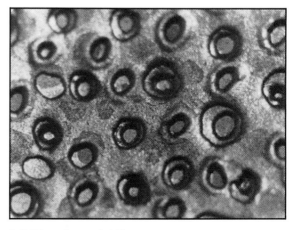

6. Built by rosin ground etching

14. Various half-tone textures made by hand and machine tools
on metal plates (magnified details)

15. Aquatint tones: Experiment by Angel Rodriquez

these pillars come under the crushing weight of the press roller. How well the pillars stand up to repeated printing depends on their individual size and how densely they are spread across the plate. In laying the ground for aquatint, we should bear in mind the following considerations:

Size of the rosin grain. We may lay grounds with many different sizes of rosin grains—from coarse grains that produce rough textures, to fine-grained ones that give velvety tones.

Density of grain distribution. If fine in size, the rosin grains should be thickly distributed on the plate. (After the etching, if the ground is finer (grayer) than desired, it can be re-aquatinted and re-bitten.) If the grains are coarser in size (resulting in a rougher texture) they may be more sparsely scattered on the plate.

Accuracy of heating. If heated to a certain point, grains of a rosin ground melt to half their volume, sitting as half-spheres on the surface of the plate. The ground produced by this degree of heating is fine and granular. If heated beyond this point, the half-grains of rosin melt and spread into worm-like and stringy shapes. The result is pure texture, not tonal gradation. One should take care in heating the ground to produce the texture one desires. Accidently overheating will cover the plate completely and leave no

bare metal for the acid to etch.

Length of time etched. Acid not only bites an aquatint straight down around the rosin grains leaving pillars of metal under them, but also bites into the sides of the pillars and weakens them if it is too strong (this effect is called *underbiting*). A weaker acid, say 1 part acid to 8 parts water, does not underbite a rosin ground much. The length of time the plate is exposed to the acid controls the tonal intensity of the aquatint. The deeper the plate is etched, the more ink it will hold. The artist can etch different parts of the aquatinted plate for different lengths of time (from 3 all the way up to 45 minutes) to produce a series of tonal gradations.

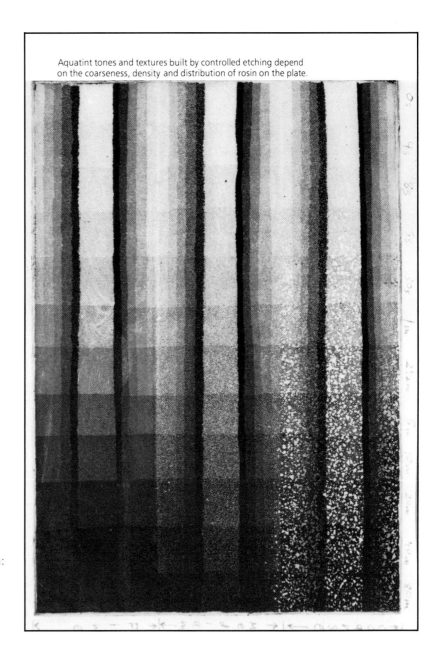

Aquatint tones and textures built by controlled etching depend on the coarseness, density and distribution of rosin on the plate.

16. Print taken from aquatint etching:
Worked by Stephen McMillan

17. Aquatint: "Self Portrait" by Marian Petit. 1984

Materials

A metal plate
Rosin powder
Stopping-out varnish

Brushes
Nitric acid
Etching needle, scraper and burnisher

Procedure

The plate should be free of grease and chemically clean:

- □ Prepare a paste of ammonia mixed with French chalk (whiting); rub this paste with a rag on the plate under a stream of cold, running water. The plate is clean when the water forms an unbroken sheet on it.

- □ Place the plate on a wire screen and sprinkle it with granulated rosin dust, shaken from a fabric bag. The finer the fabric of the bag the finer the rosin grains will be that fall from it. As a guide, the rosin should cover about 60% of the plate; in other words, enough to make the surface of the plate seem evenly white when seen at eye level.

- □ Heat the plate evenly and slowly, moving the source of heat back and forth underneath it, but never concentrating heat at any one spot.

- □ While heating the plate, examine it close to eye level. As the rosin melts its appearance will change from a white, dusted surface to a transparent, wet surface. The change is rather like the melting of frost. This is the "half-way point" of the melting rosin grains referred to earlier. Discontinue heating the plate and allow it to cool.

48

- Immerse the plate in a medium acid solution. Vary the immersion time, depending on the depth of tone desired. Make certain that the immersed plate has bubbles on its surface; this means the acid is etching.
- Remove the plate from the acid and wash it off with cold water. Wipe the plate with alcohol to remove the rosin. A trial proof may now be pulled.
- At this stage one may choose to intensify or reduce certain tonal gradations in the plate. Intensification can be done by re-aquatinting and re-biting the plate (protecting with hard-ground those areas of the plate that are meant to be intensified); or small areas of tone may be deepened with roulettes. To reduce the tone of an area, one may use the scraper on it and then burnish.

4. Relief or Deep-Etch, Open-Bite

Occasionally, during some rare moment, one becomes aware of the totality of the plate—its presence as a three dimensional object. The entire plate is now the launching point for an exciting way of building an image. William Blake's powerful relief etchings have demonstrated his deep awareness of the whole plate, its depths as well as its surfaces. He may initially have become aware of the plate as a sculptural totality while driving his burin through a copper plate. Later, he extended the three dimensional possibilities of his plates by biting them deeply with acid.

The excitement one feels in exploring the many levels of the plate is communicated in the building of the image. Trapped in one's ideas, one tends to stay on the surface of materials, exploiting them, blind to the deep possibilities of the material underneath. The very realization of the totality of the material leads one to greater sensitivity in building the image. This produces an image that is whole and strong, with all levels of the plate participating in it's creation.

18. Magnified aquatint plate (watch columns underbitten)

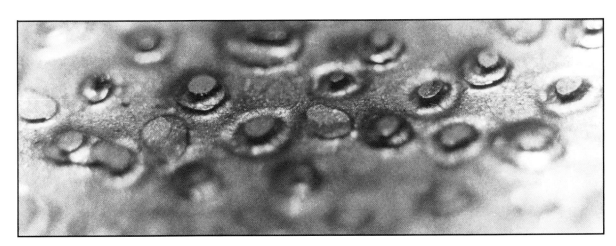

As we shall see, we can work deeply in the plate by a variety of means. With burins, gouges and scorpers we can dig deep sculptural grooves and hollows in the plate. With roulettes we can build different intensities of tone. With scrapers alone we can scrape and carve undulations, sinuous waves; and with burnishers, polish and change the tone of the waves and textures. With machine tools, we can build reliefs with cutting and gouging heads; and with various textured heads of stone and metal, we can lay textures and gradations of tone on any level of the relief plate.

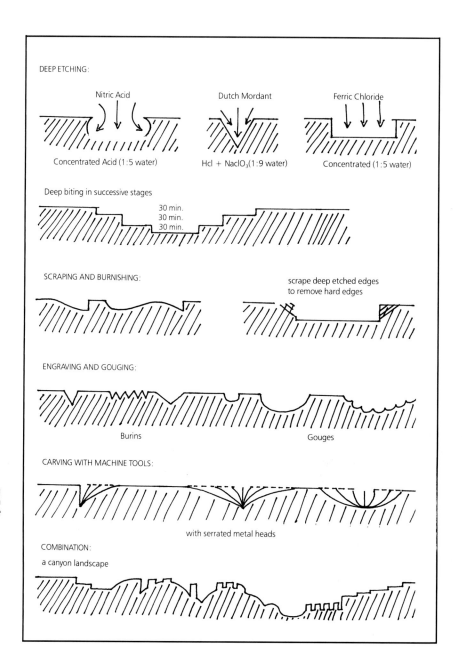

19. Diagram: Building sculptural surfaces in the plate

20. Details of relief surfaces worked by different methods

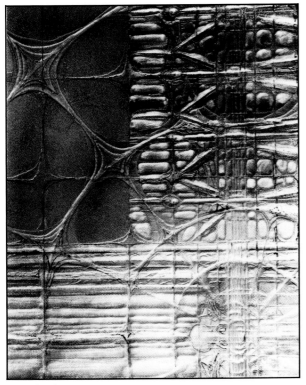

Gouged surface

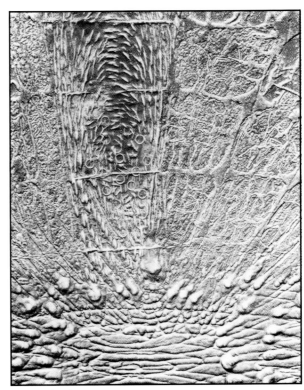

Aquatinted surface

Sanded textural surface

Carved surface

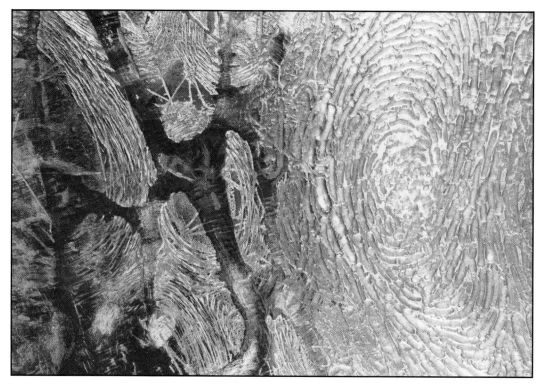

Etching, engraving and gouging

Etching and carving with hand and machine tools

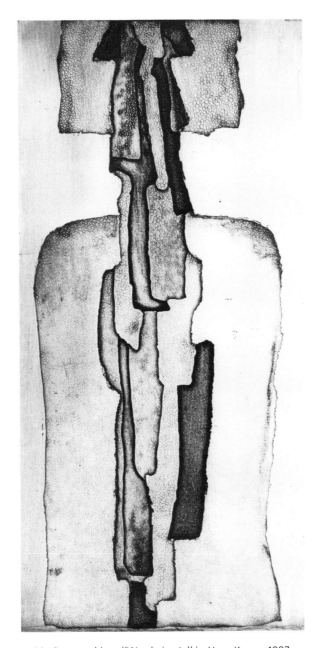

22. Deep-etching: "Wandering In" by Yung Kyung. 1987

Materials

Plate (copper or zinc)　　　　　　　　*Burnisher*
Hard-ground (liquid)　　　　　　　　 *Contact paper and masking tape*
Asphaltum (liquid)　　　　　　　　　 *Permanent felt marker*
Nitric acid　　　　　　　　　　　　　*Sharp X-acto knife*
Assorted paint brushes　　　　　　　 *Various abrasive and polishing papers*
Scraper

Procedure

□ Draw a design directly onto the plate using liquid hard ground (sometimes mixed with asphaltum to strengthen the hard-ground) and brushes of desired thicknesses.

□ Immerse the plate in a bath of strong nitric acid (1 part nitric to 5 parts of water) for about 20 to 30 minutes. Remove the plate and wash off the acid with cold, running water. Dry the plate and draw new shapes as desired with brush and hard-ground as before.

□ Re-immerse the plate in acid for 20 to 30 minutes. The steps above can be repeated 5 or 6 times to build up multiple levels of relief on the plate.

(Variation A)

□ Another method of producing deep relief surfaces is to cover the plate with self-adhesive white contact paper (to ensure adhesion, the plate may be heated slightly and the contact paper burnished down.) Draw the design on the contact paper with a permanent felt marker. Carefully cut the drawn areas with a sharp X-acto knife and peel off those areas. Bite in the acid, as above.

□ To build deeper levels, more of the contact paper can be cut away and the plate re-bitten. Repeat this procedure 5 or 6 times, to get a greater variety of depths.

(Variation B)

□ Add pieces of masking tape (instead of cutting away pieces of contact paper) between successive re-bitings. The plate can be bitten any number of times, adding more masking tape each time. Masking tape can also be used to repair or add to areas accidently cut away in the contact paper method.

□ Any surface areas left in relief by acid biting will have a hard edge, against which ink will pile up. To reduce the hardness of these edges if desired, bevel off with the scraper and smooth with the burnisher.

□ Relief surfaces in a deep-bitten plate may sometimes be changed and removed with the scraper and burnisher.

□ Now one may experiment with texturing all levels of the plate with aquatint, and again scraping and burnishing. Abrasive papers may be used to change and polish sections of the aquatinted surfaces.

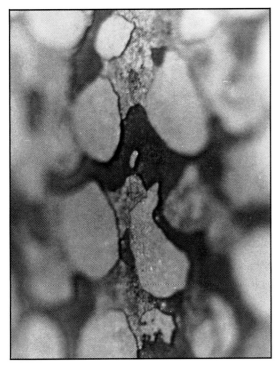

1. Etching and sanding

2. Deep etch, gouging and punching

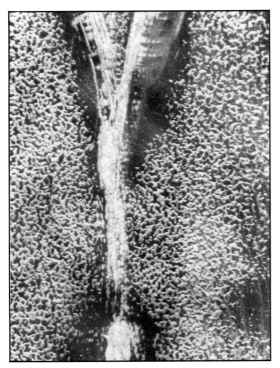

3. Deep etch, aquatint and scraping

4. Deep etch, punching and scraping

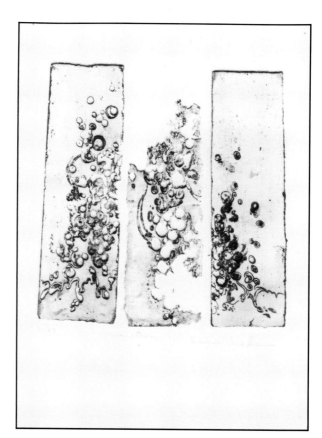

24. Deep-biting:
"Coronation" by Laura Lader. 1978

25. Relief-etching: "Spirals" by Laura Bottome. 1980

B. Tools: Hand and Machine

The most direct way of working on the plate is with hand and machine tools. This has been so from the beginning, when artists engraved metal with burins and chased it with metal punches. There is a degree of closeness, a rapport with the plate, that one achieves by working it with tools. The artist is an active part of the plate-making process when he sculpts, cuts and carves the metal with lines, textures and halftones. Instead of smothering the plate with any outside materials and techniques, as is so often done today, he brings the powerful directness and simplicity of a sculptural image into the plate.

Whereas other conventional methods of working the plate, such as surface etchings, have a tendency to lose us in the surface of the plate, tools virtually force us to dig below that surface. Inspite of ourselves we are drawn into exploring the deep totality of the plate. The plate has changed from a two-dimensional surface to a three-dimensional terrain. The entire plate is the meeting place for all these materials and tools, where ideas and images become active! Participating with the plate and various inks, rollers and papers sharpens one's sensitivity and awareness.

Time, practice and purpose have evolved the various forms of tools. The artist needs extreme sensitivity to learn to use them. He will learn a great deal by simply exploring the qualities of the different lines made by a burin, the wiry nervous line of the dry point needle, the soft halftones that can be laid down with various mezzotint roulettes and rockers. Whatever the approach taken in using these tools, the important thing is not to lose the directness and involvement that they afford in the process of building an image.

Hand tools are an extremely natural and direct form of working the image. Working with machine tools adds the extra dimension of immediacy. The speed and dynamism of machine tools brings to a plate the same immediacy as a brush to a painting. As with oil paint, the image is not lost by devoting excessive time to detailing textures or forms. These can be changed with machine tools in a short enough time that one does not lose sight of their effect on the entire image.

Machine tools, compared with traditional and conventional approaches, have brought about a total transformation in the way we work the plate.

The joy of working with machine tools is being able to create deep undulations, crevices and various degrees of textures spontaneously and easily, enhancing the intensity and graphic quality of an image. But out of lethargy or inattentiveness, one may end up content with the sheer facility machine tools offer and become a clever technician, forever getting lost in solving little puzzles of detail.

With machine tools, creation of halftones becomes an immediate and direct process. The finest tonal gradations can be realized simultaneously (in contrast to the step-by-step, time consuming halftone building by aquatint and photo-etching processes). Carving the plate with machine tools is akin to carving stone. Machine tool carving conveys to the plate much the same monumental and sculptural quality as carving gives to stone.

The three-dimensional quality of the plate is essentially linked to its interaction with rollers of different densities and inks of different viscosities, as well as with other important materials in color printmaking, as we shall see later.

The artist should learn to maintain his tools well, keeping their working surfaces sharp and covered with a thin film of machine oil to prevent rust. Each tool demands special attention according to its function.

1. Hand Tools

Materials

Burins, gouges and scorpers
Scraper
Burnisher
Dry point needle
Roulettes and rockers
Assorted chasing punches

Assorted metal files
Assorted emery papers, carborundum paper, crocus cloth
India and Arkansas stones
Machine oil and kerosene

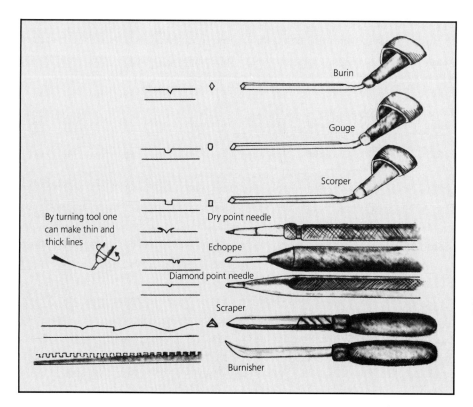

26. Diagram: Hand tools

27. Engraving: ''Portrait d'une Femme Sud Americaine'' by Jean Lodge. 1984

Burins and Gouges. Using a burin is close to drawing lines in metal, with the difference that its lines are sculptural instead of flat. The sensitivity and flexibility of the graven line gives it immense graphic quality.

The burin is a small, thin steel rod—4 or 5 inches long—with a diamond-shaped cross section; its end has been sliced off at an angle (see illustration). The working face of the burin must be kept absolutely sharp.

The burin is pushed into the metal, with an energy surging away from the body. It should be held in a relaxed but firm grip, with the energy of the entire arm pushing the tool forward. The wrist and fingers do not initiate any push, but merely guide it. Direction of the engraved line is primarily determined in two ways: for straight lines, the tool is pushed forward; for curves, the tool stays virtually motionless and the plate is rotated by the opposite hand. Lines that swell and taper are obtained by varying the degree of penetration of the burin with the metal.

The burin may also produce a variety of textures and tones. By cross-hatching it will produce a texture; by spacing the hatched lines closer together, a tone is produced. The effects of texture and tone can also be made by dotting the plate with the burin, spacing dots sparsely or closely as desired.

Gouges will hollow out U-shaped lines of a variety of widths, depending on the gouge size. The hollows will print as embossed darks or lights, depending on how much ink was left in them during wiping. Textures are obtained by holding the tool at a sharp angle to the metal and simultaneously rocking it side to side while pushing it forward.

The scraper is used to shave off slivers of metal raised by the burin and the gouge; it also has a variety of other uses described below.

Scraper. In dry point the scraper can be used to tone down or eradicate lines; in aquatint it is used in conjunction with the burnisher to control tonal gradations; and in deep-bite etching it can remove the hard edge on relief surfaces and texture various deep-bitten levels. However, the scraper may also be used alone to create reliefs (deep and shallow) and surface textures. The scraper has the advantage of being able to sculpt reliefs with gently sloping and curving sides, which are hard to obtain using any other methods except machine tools.

Burnisher. The function of the burnisher is to smooth down the rough surfaces left by the scraper. One may burnish scraped surfaces almost to a high polish or leave some medium degree of scraped texture, which will print gray. In aquatint or mezzotint, the burnisher is the main tool for drawing light and shades out of the dark ground. It is capable of building an extraordinary range of tones.

The surface of the burnisher must be kept highly polished. The burnisher is always used lubricated with machine grease or Vaseline. Used unlubricated, it will scratch the plate severely, as well as itself.

Dry Point Needle. Dry point is a medium that appears easier than it actually is. It is difficult simultaneously to exert the pressure and exercise the control required by a dry point line. This requires both involvement and sensitivity. The needle acts directly on the plate with its point only, having no cutting edge to decrease the resistance as it scratches through the metal. The needle leaves a burr along the scratch, and when the plate is inked the burr holds a certain amount of ink, giving the line a soft, blurry quality in the final print. The burr is extremely soft; under the enormous pressure of the press, it wears away after comparatively few impressions. The soft character of the dry point lines thus is soon lost.

Dry point can be used to augment tonal values in etching, and when cross-hatched gives powerful tonal gradations.

Roulettes and Rockers. Roulettes are textured steel cylinders or cones revolving on a shaft set within their long axis. A wide variety of roulette textures and sizes are available. They may be rolled directly over the surface of the plate to imprint their texture and the resultant strokes crossed by other strokes to produce gradations of tone. Different kinds of roulettes can be superimposed on an area of the plate to intensify the depth of their tones. Roulette textures can be burnished down to create beautiful contrasts of light and shade. The roulette can also be used to restore burnished-off aquatint textures.

The rocker is a tool with a crescent shaped, toothed edge, which works in a fashion similar to that of the roulette. The rocker is rocked over the plate, laying down single rows of dots; these strokes are criss-crossed over each other many times. When inked during printing, this ground produces beautiful velvety darks. One builds light areas in a mezzotint ground by burnishing them.

28. Hand and machine tools used in working the plate

2. Machine Tools

Materials

Attachments for electric drills
  1) *Flexible sander discs (with emery and sandpapers cut to fit)*
  2) *Rubber sander discs*
  3) *Wire brushes (assorted)*
  4) *Saw discs*
  5) *Rasping and filing discs*
  6) *Felt and cloth buffing wheels*
Flexible shafts: Holding maximum size 1/8'' and 1/4'' tool stem

Assorted disc and wheel heads: For cutting, filing, sanding and polishing
Metal heads (assorted): For carving, gouging, cutting, grinding, filing and texturing
Stone heads (assorted): For texturing, sanding and grinding
Foredom hanging motor: For flexible shaft (with optional foot pedal on-off speed control)
Flexible shaft attachments: Short shafts (called arbours and mandrels) for holding disc and wheel attachments; 3/32" in diameter.

One can also buy a second-hand motor with a chuck and 2 flexible shafts accepting tool stems of 1/8" and 1/4" maximum diameter. Check that motor operation is fairly quiet.

Procedure

Machine tools demand of us that we work the plate using sculptural methods. We must explore the deep spaces of the plate as sculpture. The entire plate may be worked in lines, hollows, reliefs, crisp edges and soft, undulating forms. Textures and tonal values take on new meaning as well.

  □ Using various metal cutting heads (such as disc cutters), create linear structures and cut away various areas of the plate.

61

- Using inverted cone cutters, carve V-shaped valleys.
- Using conical heads, scrape down textures in deep levels and on surface reliefs. Bevel the sides of acid-bitten reliefs. This cutter can create slanting, flat areas.
- Rounded conical heads and spherical serrated heads can carve U-shaped hollows, undulating structures and deep valleys.
- Texture burrs come in a variety of shapes and surface textures, which pit the plate in various depths. Burrs can produce simple textures or a wide range of tonal gradations—increasing or decreasing the density and the depth of the pits.
- Stone grinding heads are available in India stone and carborundum in a wide variety of shapes and sizes. They are excellent for creating delicate gray tones.
- Sanding and polishing discs, which screw onto small tool shanks, are good for texturing or polishing small crevices and linear structures.
- Large sanding machines, rather than flexible shaft tools, are used to polish and grain bigger areas of the plate.
- Electric drills with sanding and polishing attachments function much like sanding machines, but they can be tilted to create gradations of textures and tones.

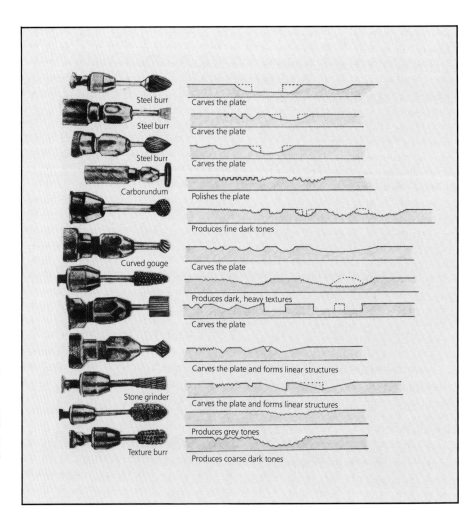

29. Diagram: Machine tools

Flexible shaft tool:
a motor-driven flexible shaft
with serrated metal heads,
carborundum or stone grinders and
various textured metal heads to cut
halftone structures in the plate.

30. Etching by photo-process:
"I Was Only Five Then" by
Yoko Takahashi. 1984

C. Photo-Processes

Photo-processes offer a tremendous challenge to the artist. Photographic images, such as collages, can be integrated into a powerful graphic statement. It is, however, difficult to combine them effectively with structures produced by other processes—for example, aquatint, deep bites or tooled areas—to create a piece with graphic unity.

Although photo-processes are not a quick and easy substitute for other methods, they should be respected for the unique effects they are able to produce. The excitement of using photo-processes consists of building a structured, integrated image from many other images, building up to a powerful statement. From collected photographic images, we communicate statements in a visual language that is at once immediate and understood. Or the photographic image, viewed in an extremely close-up or unfamiliar way, can lead us to new concepts of abstraction.

Building halftones by photo-processes further expands the territory that the artist can explore. He can deep-bite a whole range of tonal gradations into a photo-halftone plate by biting it from 3 to 45 minutes in selected areas. This enables him to intensify the color and texture of the print. These effects may be modified by working over areas with scraper and burnisher to build tone, as in aquatint and mezzotint.

63

1. Photo Image Building

Materials

Metal plate (copper or zinc) with beveled
 corners and edges
Kodak KPR photo-resist liquid
Kodak KPR photo-resist developer
Kodak KPR photo-resist dye
Lacquer thinner (or KPR stripper)

Acetate photo-copy of photographs/pen
 drawings
Actual positives from Kodak Ortho Film
 Type 3 (Kodaliths)
Acids: Nitric, Dutch Mordant or Ferric
 Chloride

Procedure

- Prepare the elements to be transferred to the plate: black and white photographs, actual size or enlargements, and pen drawings are photocopied onto acetate. Prior to transfer, the various elements may be formed into a collage, cutting and overlapping as the composition requires, or used separately for desired placement directly onto the plate. The emulsion side of these negatives may also be drawn and scratched into with a drypoint needle.
- Thoroughly degrease the plate with ammonia and whiting.
- Sensitize the plate: standing it on one edge in a tray, at an angle of slightly less than 90 degrees, carefully pour KPR photo-resist liquid along the length of the top edge. Allow the liquid to flow down the plate, eventually forming an even, continuous coating. Alternatively, the liquid may be poured onto the plate and centrifuged.
- Set the sensitized plate in an area to dry, protected from direct light.
- When the surface is completely dry, place the negatives flat on the plate, emulsion side to plate surface.
- Place the plate in a vacuum table to be exposed. The time of exposure depends upon the type of light used—pulsed Xenon lamp, Mercury vapor lamp or photographic flood lights.
- Develop the plate in KPR photo-resist developer.
- Rinse the plate and cover it with a thin film of KPR photo-resist dye. This will show the image in blue.
- Immerse the plate in a relatively weak solution of nitric acid (1:8 to 1:25). If deep bite is required, and therefore use of a stronger acid, heat the plate until the blue surface turns brown. This will harden the resist (and also make the plate more difficult to clean) and raise its tolerance to the acid. Various portions of the plate may be protected by stop-out varnish or liquid hard ground in between a series of immersions to create a range of levels in the plate. Drawing through or scratching away parts of the resist and then biting will also add dimension to the image. One

- may experiment with textures scratched through the ground with a dry point needle and various roulettes.
- Hand and machine tools may also be used to develop reliefs and textures and tonal gradations at any point, either before or after the resist has been removed. (This depends on whether one wishes to bite the plate further with acid).
- At any stage, a trial print may be pulled without cleaning off the photo-resist dye.
- When acid work is finished, clean the plate with lacquer thinner or KPR stripper.
- This technique presents a health hazard, as all of the KPR chemicals, as well as the lacquer thinner, are toxic. They should be used in an extremely well-ventilated area while wearing a protective filter mask (with organic vapour cartridge) and gloves.

31. Photo-processes: "Landscapes" by Jill Enfield. 1984

2. Photo-Halftones

Materials

Same as Photo Imaging Building materials, (Sec. I) with the following additions:
Halftone screens of various line densities

Thin sheet of frosted transparent glass or plastic
Acetate photo-copies of various textures

65

Procedure

- Same as in Sec.I for sensitizing and developing the plate. The images being developed here, rather than photo line images, are halftones and textures or photo-images combined with halftones and textures.
- Gauze or transparent net fabrics can also be used to develop textures on the plate, by covering the plate with them and exposing the plate directly to the light source.
- Like mezzotinted or aquatinted plates, photo-halftone plates may be worked with scraper and burnisher to generate different gradations and tones.
- One may want to experiment with hand and machine tools on a developed photo plate to create deep reliefs and textures.

D. Combination Processes

All of these processes (or a few of them together) for working the plate—the acid and tool processes, etc.—can be combined on one plate to build the image. The making of an image on a plate can occur in so many ways; each process, combined with any other, opens up rich possibilities. The combinations are innumerable.

As with any freedom, however, responsibility comes close behind. The artist discerns that the force driving him to create is the image: at once the stimulus, need and focus for his expression. The materials and processes bring the image to its fullest development, without which it is meaningless. The entire approach to materials and processes should be informed by the understanding that, together with the image, they form an indivisible whole.

Through carelessness, one can be led to emphasize one of these elements at the expense of others. Image cannot exist in its fullest, most expressive form without materials and processes; on the other hand, materials and processes have a life of their own, and do not exist solely to be exploited by the image. The unity of materials, processes and image is of paramount importance.

The enormous number of possibilities inherent in combination processes leads to another possibility—that of getting side-tracked or overwhelmed by the complexities of materials and techniques. We may become lost in a maze of techniques, later to emerge as craftsmen, claiming we have mastered materials.

Whatever the approach taken in moving toward a deeper understanding of materials and processes, it should be a positive one—full of curiosity, experiment and learning.

The experience of working with each of the methods and becoming familiar with a wide range of materials gives the artist an increasingly rich means of expressing his images. Combining, eliminating, recombining, he may find a particular set of techniques and materials that fit his particular plate.

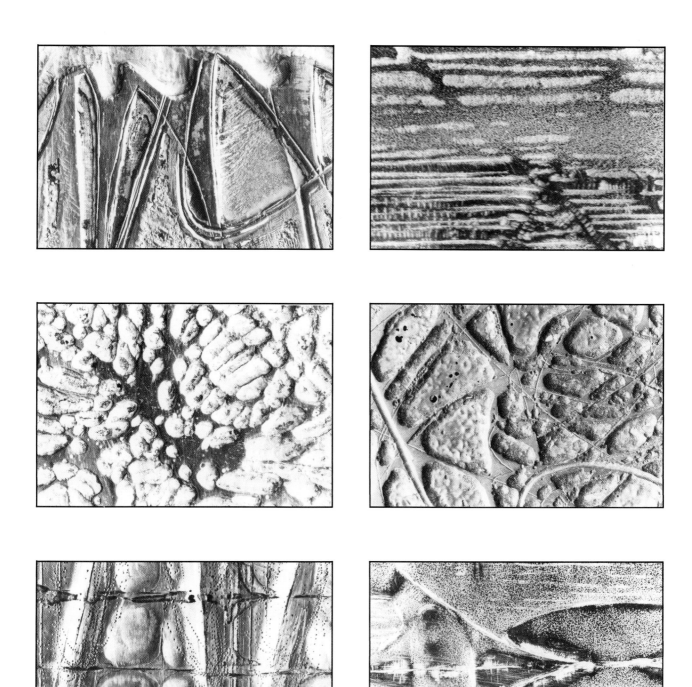

32. Enlarged details of completed plates
(worked by etching, engraving and carving)

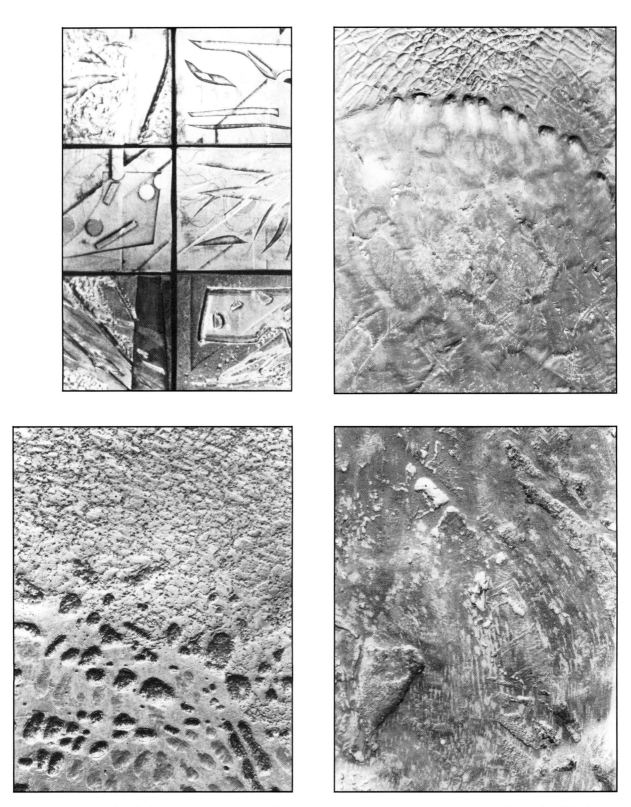

33. Details of plates built by combination processes (by deep biting, scraping, gouging, aquatinting, sanding and polishing)

34. Soft ground textures:
"Transparencies" by Jane Walentas. 1983

Trial and error and continuous exploration will open his path and lead to further discovery of new ways and new materials. There are no rigid formulas to be followed. The combined processes described below are those that I have found useful; they suggest some of the possibilities of approaching a plate.

1) With a felt-tip Flomaster pen and children's wax crayons, draw on an unbitten plate or on an aquatint surface.

2) Using asphaltum grounds or plastic glues, develop a series of deep bites in the plate. Then lay various tonal gradations of aquatint on the different deep bitten levels. As above, draw on the various aquatints with Flomaster pen and wax crayons, and develop them as broad, linear structures in various tones. With a machine grinder, remove all the hard edges of the crevices, creating undulating, wavy surfaces. Engrave the plate with a burin or build ravine-like, gouged linear depths and emphasize the areas with deep acid-bitten textured surfaces.

3) Using photo-processes, transfer a photographic image, built of halftones, onto a plate and rework the image with further acid biting, and hand and machine tools.

4) Lay halftone on a zinc plate and bite it in nitric acid. Remove the emulsion and work the composition. With further acid work, some of the tones disappear in a more concentrated acid. With serrated machine grinders and vibro-tools, reliefs, textures and various intensities of halftones can be built.

5) Using a dry point needle and a metal ruler, structure the surface of the plate with the drawing in straight lines; with a vibro tool, build the images in different tones and textures.

69

35. Lift ground etching:
''Movement'' by Ibrahim Ibrahim. 1978

36. Author at the printing press

37. Students working with inks and rollers.

7 Color Printmaking: Materials and Processes

The Materials

Printmaking involves—besides plates, printing inks and papers—tools, oils, varnishes, acids, solvents, rollers, printing presses and other equipment. Each one of these materials is continuous and possesses a range of variations that cannot be quantified. We must have an involved, sensitive mind, able to visualize the inner workings of materials and their interrelationships. Only if we are willing to experience and experiment with materials can we integrate them into the printmaking process.

Inquiring into materials, we should study the various inks, rollers and papers involved in color printmaking. Then, inspired by our images, we must begin to explore the viscosity process and other methods of simultaneous intaglio and surface color printmaking.

Where color printmaking is involved, the innumerable variations of colors, of treatment of the surfaces and depths of the plate, pose a challenge to the artist. Without the drive to integrate and simplify printmaking processes, and to gain a deeper understanding of the nature of colors and how they interact, one can easily become lost in complexities of technique. The artist should learn to develop his image through the innumerable ways of working with these materials, without ceasing his search for directness and simplicity of expression. It is through this search that exploration and discovery happen.

Their Nature and Behavior

To be really effective in the use of inks in color printmaking, we must develop a closeness with the world of colors; we have to understand the behavior of color on a molecular level. On this level we see solid pigment particles in cooked linseed oil as resembling brightly colored pebbles suspended in a meshwork of dry, transparent strings. The polymers of the cooked oil are the strands of the meshwork. They are heaped up, matted, transparent fibers that surround the particles of pigment—the pebbles we spoke of earlier. How pure and transparent the polymer fibers of the oil are will determine how well the color shows through.

Like most solids, pigments have a crystalline structure with several molecules held in a specific chemical shape. The character of each pigment particle—whether it is angular or rounded, whether it has smooth surfaces or rough or broken ones, whether it is pure or covered with impurities—will determine the brightness and brilliance of the color. How heavily the meshwork is charged with pigment particles will determine the color's luminosity and intensity. The color particles must not break up or dissolve in the oil, or they will stain the entire meshwork. This is what happens when a dyestuff (which is made of single molecules) is added to the oil meshwork.

The thinnest deposit of color that we can lay on the surface of a glass plate will be a meshwork no thicker than one layer of pigment particles. This we call a film.

When we roll one film of color over another, we increase the concentration of pigment, thus increasing the intensity of the color. If each film is of a different color, the different pigment particles will juxtapose as color mixtures of great richness.

In contrast to offset colors, intaglio colors contain a large quantity of pigment (up to 80% in proportion to the oil). Since the ink has to fill deep crevices in the plate, it must have a certain stiffness and body, which is given to it by the extra pigment. Intaglio colors look darker than offset colors because of the large amount of pigment.

Their Interactions

We must be aware, when we structure these films of color simultaneously on a plate, of the depths and surfaces of that plate. The intaglio parts take intaglio inks, which are rubbed into them; the relief surfaces are rolled with offset inks. As the intaglio inks, which occupy the deep crevices of the plate, are more plentiful than the surface rolled inks, the artist must learn to balance the two so they combine harmoniously. The intensity of the intaglio can be increased by charging it with powder color; or bring it closer to the surface color by reducing it with a transparent white base.

By using rollers of different densities (hard, medium and soft) and knowing how to control the viscosity of each color with uncooked linseed oil, we can superimpose or juxtapose layers of colors at any and all levels of the plate. The use of uncooked linseed oil to control viscosity is the key factor here; this is only understood after experimenting with and learning the nature and behavior of oils.

With the combination of intaglio and surface colors through viscosity, one can achieve a print with a single pass through the press, as in black and white prints. If the colors are laid out properly, with the correct organization, the whole process of pulling the print will take only a few minutes. The tremendous simplicity and directness of this process bring the artist closer to the medium of printmaking. With some degree of understanding and sensitivity to materials and their interactions, an artist can print his own edition. He will derive more excitement from being involved directly in this way. The commercial printer, who depends heavily on analysis and measurement, will find this process not easily within his scope; it is organic and not fully analyzable.

1. Printing Inks

Printing inks are mixtures of pigments or powder colors and a cooked linseed oil. There are numerous types of printing ink, which contain different proportions of pigment and oil, depending on their intended use. The simultaneous printmaking process requires the combined use of intaglio and offset printing inks to achieve its rich color effects—with intaglio inks applied to the depths of the plate and the offset inks to its surface. These two types of inks have quite different compositions and properties.

Intaglio inks have a large volume of pigment (about 80%) in relation to the volume of oil. Offset inks, in contrast to the intaglio colors, have about 20% volume of pigment; the remainder of the mixture is oil. The pigment is of fine particle size and dispersed evenly in the ink; it should be made of non-bleeding powder colors, otherwise the pigment particles will separate from the vehicle and float on the surface.

Before adding a given pigment to an ink mixture, the ink manufacturer reduces its particle size as much as possible. The fine pigment particles are then mixed with oil and dispersed throughout it by being repeatedly passed through the rollers of special "ink-grinding" machines. (Note: pigment particles cannot be reduced below a certain size by grinding. The grinding machine mentioned here and the artist's hand-grinding of pigment in ink only increase the dispersion of pigment in the ink; they do not grind it further).

The composition and viscosity of the inks differ not only from one manufacturer to another but also between the colors themselves. Inks also differ in different areas of printmaking, such as serigraphy, lithography, relief and offset printing, etc. In the simultaneous intaglio and surface color printmaking processes, litho offset inks are preferable because of their transparency, which makes it possible to superimpose color layers.

Pigments or Powder Colors

Pigments used today are salts of certain metals. Many metal salts have beautiful colors, but comparatively few of them can be used in inks and artist's paints owing to their chemical instability and impermanence. Prior to the nineteenth century and its advances

38. Cabinet with bottles of powder inks and hand rollers

in both organic and inorganic chemistry, most pigments were from natural sources, both organic and inorganic.

Pigments of Natural Origin: Natural Inorganic Colors. Minerals in the earth are the sources of the naturally occurring inorganic pigments, in which iron oxide is the usual color producer. Red oxides, ochres, raw siennas, raw umbers and terra verts can be used as pigments with little alteration beyond drying and sifting for impurities. Changes in the coloration of these pigments take place when they are calcined (oxidized) or roasted, by heating in the dry process, or by controlling rusting in the wet process. During these synthetic treatments, water is removed and the color becomes darker and more red. Burnt Sienna and Burnt Umber are achieved in this way. Cinnabar (a reddish ore of mercury), Chrysacolla (a green ore of copper) and Ultramarine (the precious blue gem Lapis Lazuli) are other examples of natural pigments.

Natural Organic Colors. Organic compounds develop around a carbon base which is the building block of living material. These include pigments made from dyes derived exclusively from animal and vegetable sources. Some examples of these are: Carmine (a fugitive red color made from the dye extracted from the Central American cochineal insect), Carthame (another fugitive red made from dried petals of the safflower plant), Tyrian or Royal Purple (a dye highly prized in ancient Greece, extracted from shellfish of the genus Murex), Indian Yellow (cow urine), Indigo (indigo plants) and Sepia (ink sac extract of cuttle fish). Some of these natural dyes are still available today, but are not used much as artist's colors because of their impermanence. Several blacks are obtained by burning organic substances and collecting the soot for use as pigment. Bone Black, Vine Black and Lamp Black are examples of such colors.

Factory Produced or Chemical Colors. Most pigments today are chemically produced. Under this heading come some natural earth pigments that are baked at a high temperature (calcined) to enhance their chemical and color stability. Some artificial pigments also undergo calcination.

The most important artificial pigments are: Cadmium Yellows and Oranges (Cadmium Sulfur salts), Cobalt Blues and Greens (Cobalt Oxides), Mars Reds and Blacks (Red and Black Oxides of iron), Chrome Oranges, Reds and Yellows (Lead-Chromium salts). By wet processes or solution methods more intense colors are obtained.

Colors from Synthetic Dyes and Metallo-Organic Colors. Most dyes in use at present are artificially manufactured. They are complex organic (carbon containing) compounds. Principally, dye molecules derive from certain aromatic hydrocarbons (carbon-hydrogen compounds) that are combined to produce multiple ring structures. These structures are modified by the addition of atoms of nitrogen and hydrogen, which give them a brilliant range of colors. These dyes, which are known as *aniline, anthracene* and *napthalene* dyes, were once widely used in fabric-dyeing and in printing, but their tendency to bleach out in strong light soon made them obsolete. They were replaced by the AZO dyes, which have become the most important coloring materials in commercial printing: among them are the famous Hansa Yellows, Benzidine Yellows and Rubine Reds. They are brilliant, powerfully staining colors, with good resistance to bleaching-out in strong sunlight.

Another recent technological discovery is the metallo-organic colors—dye-like organic molecules that are bonded to a metal atom. Of these the most widely used are the copper or iron-based phthalocyanine colors, which give a range of brilliant, deep blues and greens. They combine the intense color purity and solubility in oil of the dyes with the stability of the metallic salt pigments. Dyes, being of a molecular nature, dissolve easily in an oil vehicle, staining its entire network.

Lakes or Precipitated Dye Stuffs. Dyes have to be made into solid pigments before they are used in printing inks. Dyes are absorbed or fixed onto finely ground particles of alumina hydrate, calcium carbonate, silicate compounds or clays. The physical properties of dyes change upon being mixed with these particles; they become effectively pigment particles, able to be dispersed evenly in oil. The resulting printing inks are called lakes.

Extenders and Stabilizers. Extenders and stabilizers are white powders with no coloring power and practically transparent in oil. They are added to printing inks to improve their texture and body without altering their color. Commonly used extenders and stabilizers include Alumina Hydrate, Magnesium Carbonate, Calcium Carbonate (French Chalk) and Barium Sulphate (Blanc-Fixe). They are especially necessary in hot and humid conditions to control the ink, or to absorb excess oil added to the ink.

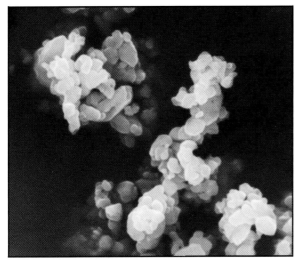

1. Cadmium red crystals (26,000x)

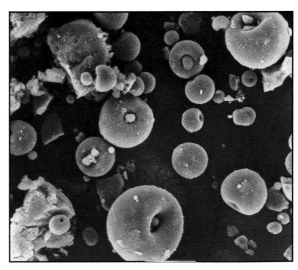

2. Milori blue pigment particles (960x)

3. Golden ochre crystals (30,000x)

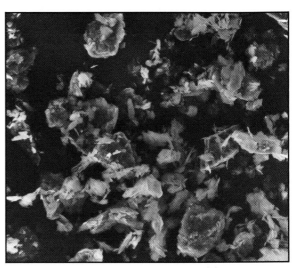

4. French chalk powder (1440x)

5. Magnesium carbonate particles (30,000x)

39. Magnified color pigments

Oils are obtained from vegetable, animal and mineral sources. Some oils dry and become tough films when exposed to air, heat and/or light; these "drying oils" serve as vehicles to carry the pigment particles and also to bind the pigment to the printing paper. Linseed oil is the most commonly used oil in intaglio and offset printing inks, although other vegetable oils, such as poppy and safflower, also have drying properties. As a liquid, linseed oil allows the pigment to flow properly. On drying, the oil polymerizes and forms a somewhat flexible film holding the pigment to the paper. The film does not crack or become brittle as it dries over time.

Linseed Oil. Linseed oil is pressed from the seeds of the flax plant, often under pressure. Steam heating forces 80% of the oil from the seed, but the result is yellowish and impure. It can be used after further processing and purification. Cold-pressed linseed oil—oil extracted directly from raw seeds—is superior, but expensive, as only 20% of the oil is taken from the seed. Raw linseed oil is used to dilute or decrease the viscosity of ink during printing. Uncooked oil easily penetrates the ink, works around its dry oil polymers to make them move or flow more easily. For use as a vehicle, giving ink the vital properties of viscosity and adhesiveness (tack), linseed oil is changed by heating into a thicker form.

Polymerization. The basic molecular (monomer) form of linseed oil is as a single unit fat molecule. When exposed to the atmosphere—to air, heat and light—these free molecules begin to join with each other to form into chains (polymers), changing the oil into a thicker form. When raw oil is heated up to 300 degrees C and exposed to air, its free molecules absorb oxygen and begin to lock into each other through the atoms of oxygen, forming a tough, thin flexible chain—a polymer. At this stage the oil is only made of short polymers—#00 plate oil. Prolonged heating forms longer polymer chains. Stopping at different stages of the polymerization process gives a range of varnishes of advancing viscosities. If the oil is heated longer, as many as 12,000 molecules can lock up, forming long string-like chains. As its individual molecules link up, the heat-treated linseed oil becomes heavy and syrupy in consistency and develops the properties of viscosity and tackiness.

Viscosity is the cohesive force, or inward pull, developed by the polymer chains. At the same time, there is a second property—tackiness (stickiness or adhesivity)—of the oil that causes it to bind or adhere to other materials such as paper, zinc or copper plates, rollers, glass slabs, etc. The longer the polymer formation the more viscous and tacky the oil becomes. These properties become very useful in the simultaneous structuring of both intaglio and surface colors on the plate. By understanding these qualities more closely, one can pile up simultaneously on the same plate up to 50 colors by various combination methods.

Gouge   Drypoint needle

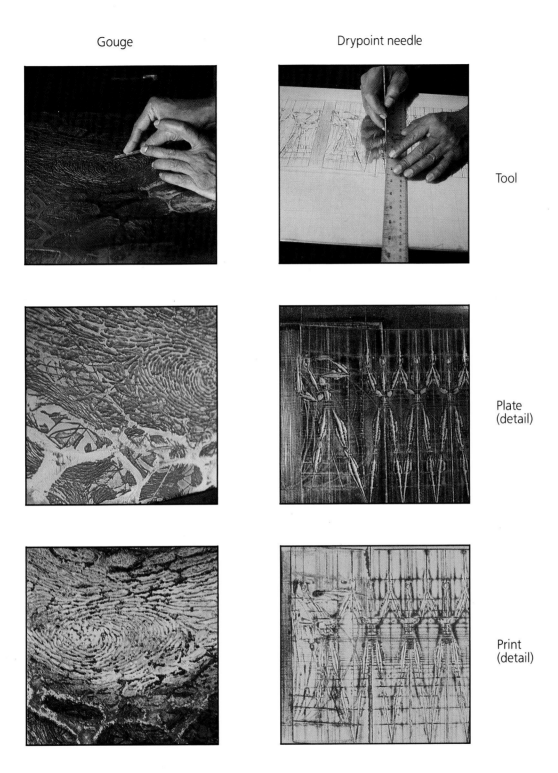

Tool

Plate
(detail)

Print
(detail)

1. Working the plate with gouge and drypoint needle, and their effect on the print.

Burnisher   Scraper

Tool

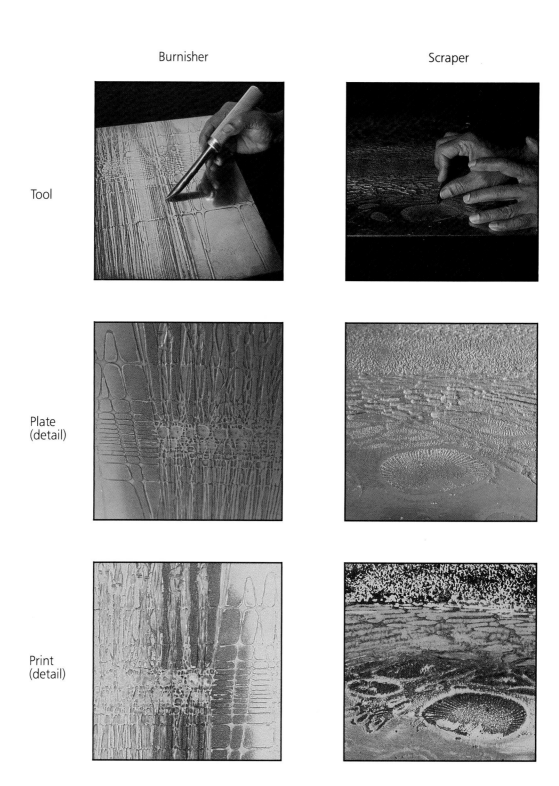

Plate
(detail)

Print
(detail)

2. Working with burnisher and scraper, and their effect on the print.

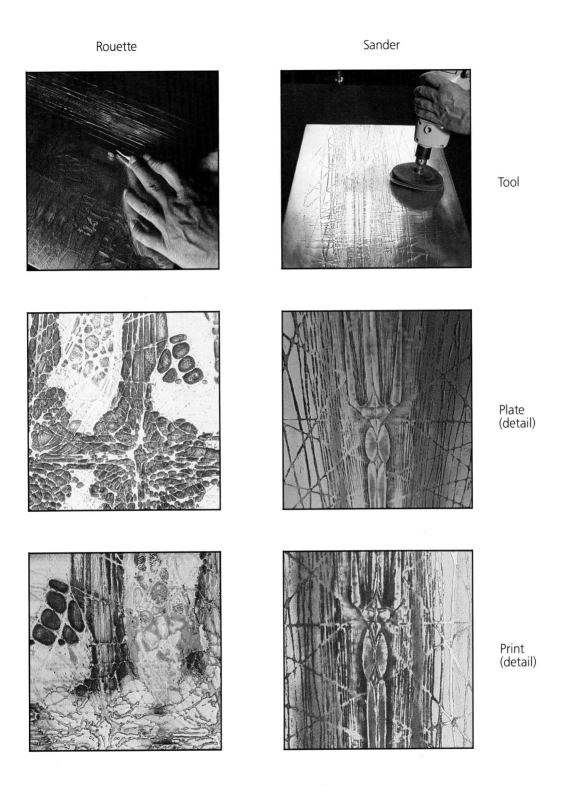

Rouette   Sander

Tool

Plate
(detail)

Print
(detail)

3. Working with roulette and sander, and their effect on the print.

Stone grinder   Conical head

Tool

Plate
(detail)

Print
(detail)

4. Working with machine tools, and their effect on the print.

Vibro tool   Metal head

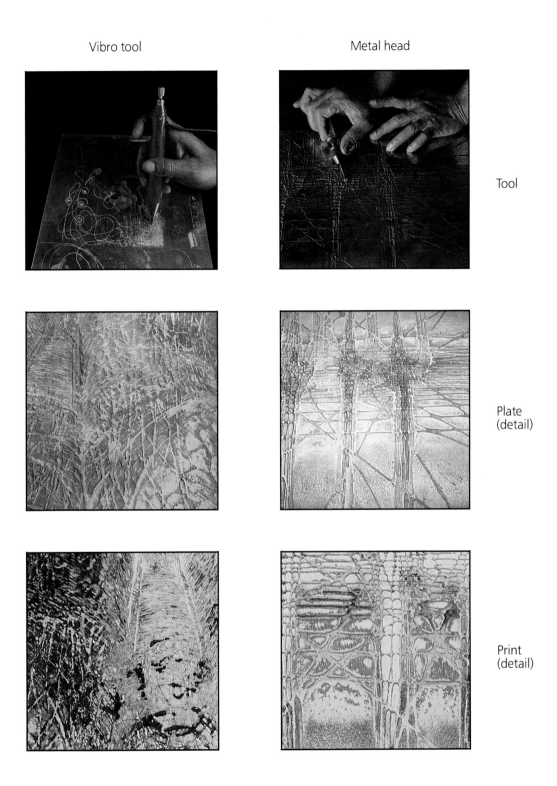

Tool

Plate
(detail)

Print
(detail)

5. Working with a vibro-tool and a round serrated metal head, and their effect on the print.

Superimposing Colors

Juxtaposing Colors

Rolling blue color

Adding more oil to blue color

Rolling yellow color over blue

Rolling blue color over yellow

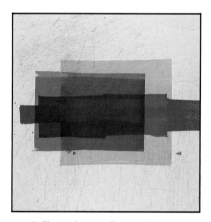

Rolling red over yellow and blue

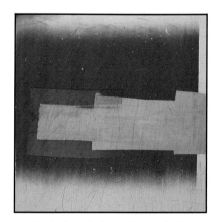

Red color rolled over blue and yellow

6. Demonstrations in viscosity processes. Color layers rolled over one another on a glass slab create color mixtures or separated color areas, depending on their various viscosities.

Microcline Feldspar

Rhodochrosite

Cerussite

Malachite

Magnetite Crystals

Wulfenite Crystals on Calcite

7. An assortment of macro structures of some color crystals.

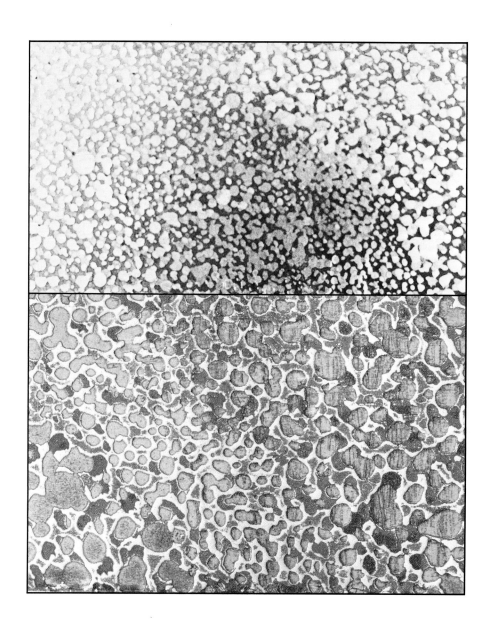

8. Magnified halftone structure on the plate and its effect on the print.

A POISON TREE.

I was angry with my friend;
I told my wrath, my wrath did end.
I was angry with my foe:
I told it not, my wrath did grow.

And I waterd it in fears,
Night & morning with my tears:
And I sunned it with smiles,
And with soft deceitful wiles.

And it grew both day and night,
Till it bore an apple bright.
And my foe beheld it shine,
And he knew that it was mine.

And into my garden stole,
When the night had veild the pole;
In the morning glad I see;
My foe outstretch'd beneath the tree.

9. *William Blake:* Detail of "A Poison Tree" from "Songs of Innocence and Experience," 1789. Collection, The Metropolitan Museum of Art, N.Y. Etched in relief and printed in color by a method of transfer.

10. *Stanley William Hayter:* "Couple," 1952. Paris, Private collection. Printed by intaglio and simultaneous use of stencil surface colors.

11. *Joan Miro:* ''Joan Miro,'' 1947. (Poem by Ruthven Todd.) Collection, The New York Public Library. Printed by intaglio simultaneously rolled with a surface layer of rainbow colors.

12. *Rolf Nesch:* "Arrow Flower," 1952-53. Oslo. Collection, The Brooklyn Museum, N.Y. Printed by combination processes.

13. *Max Ernst:* Frontispiece for André Breton's "Le Chateau Etoile," 1936. Collection, The New York Public Library. Color frottage.

14. *Krishna Reddy:* One of a series of color experiments printed by simultaneous process from a carved intaglio plate, ''The Great Clown,'' detail, (36" x 48"), 1986. Collection, Galerie Borjeson, Malmo.

Engraving the copper plate with a burin.

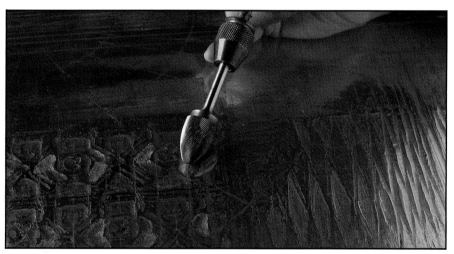

Carving the plate with a bud-shaped grinder.

Textures worked by machine tools in a metal plate.

15. Ways of engraving and carving.

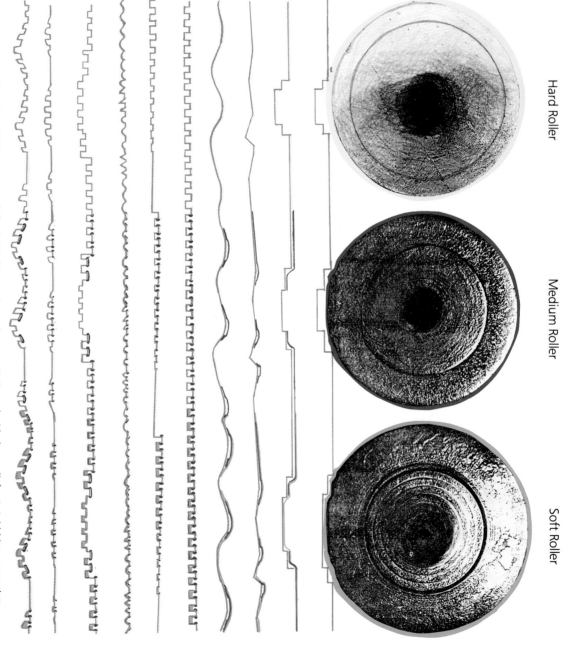

Hard Roller

Medium Roller

Soft Roller

1.

2.

3.

4.

5.

6.

7.

8.

9.

16. *Plate Cross Section:* 1. Acid-bitten deep reliefs; 2. Machine tool angular cuts; 3. Carved with deep reliefs; 4. Acid-bitten aquatint; 5. Acid-bitten aquatint scraped; 6. Textures created by machine tools; 7. Aquatints developed on acid-bitten deep reliefs; 8. A carved plate with aquatint and planed with a machine sander until the overall flatness of the plate is achieved; 9. Aquatints developed on an undulating carved surface: the surface is removed using a block sander.

Resins are used to increase the adhesion of oil-pigment films to various supports (paper, canvas, etc.). Natural resins are the hardened saps or other secretions of trees, specifically those substances that dissolve in oil, alcohol or turpentine. Examples are damar, mastic, sandarac, shellac and copal. Natural resins are not often used for artist's materials, because they do not adhere well and their dried films crack and darken with age. An exception is rosin (a secretion of pine trees), which is used as a size for paper, to limit its absorbency and improve its wet strength.

Artificial resins are polymer molecules made of linked esters (an ester is an organic salt). One ester polymer (or polyester), whose ester units are made of an alcohol with three reactive groups, has found particular use in printmaking (see illustration). This alkyd (for alcohol-acid combined) polymer is then attached to long-chain polymers of linseed oil molecules. The result is an alkyd resin, which when mixed into ink causes it to dry much faster than linseed oil or varnish, and with a thinner, tougher, more adhesive and flexible film. Colors in such resin-containing inks appear darker and glossier, since the resin wets them better than straight linseed oil.

Resins find wide use as an additive in commercial printing inks; they modify the adhesivity, film toughness and glossiness of ink. Resins are necessary to cause commercial inks to adhere firmly to the glossy, impermeable surface of commercial paper. It is important for the artist-printmaker to be aware of the properties of resin, for two reasons. First, offset inks containing resins are used in the viscosity process. Second, the structure of the paper by an artist-printer differs from that of a commercial paper. Handmade rag paper, for example, has the structure of a fine network; ink is absorbed into this network and becomes part of it while drying. Under these conditions, ink does not need the additional adhesivity resin provides; in fact, resin-containing inks can interfere with proper absorption of subsequent ink layers into the paper.

2. Ink Rollers

With the development of relief plates, rollers of different density became essential to roll ink onto the various levels of the plate. The varying degrees of density of the rollers play a major part in the printing process. To spread the color on a glass slab evenly requires being able to pick up a color film of the correct thickness onto the roller; the roller should be small enough to be handled easily, no more than 5″ to 6″ in diameter and between 20″ and 24″ in length.

- rollers of different densities are used to lay films of colors on different relief levels of the plate: soft rollers deposit ink on the deepest level of the plate; hard rollers deposit ink only on the surface.
- rollers for color printing are made of gelatin or composition, rubber, or plastic.

- gelatin or composition rollers are easily affected by temperature change and by moisture, becoming hard in cold weather and very soft in hot weather; they are damaged by absorbing moisture. A gelatin roller is so soft that it reaches the deepest levels in a relief plate which the other rollers cannot.
- rubber rollers are an improvement over the composition rollers in stability and durability; they are made of different grades, from soft to hard between 15 and 50 degrees, a durometer reading.
- polyurethane rollers are in many ways superior to other rollers being more resistant to mechanical damage and solvents.

3. Papers

As one of the basic materials in printmaking, paper plays a unique and active role and deserves to be considered in its own right as well as in relation to the other materials involved. Printmaking itself is rather like a meeting at which inks, rollers, plate and paper are all present. Understanding of this complex interplay can be greatly helped by a knowledge of the inherent characteristics of each kind of material. Therefore before questioning the response of the paper to the variety of elements with which it comes into contact, one should first consider its structure and some of its peculiarities.

The history of paper making—from its origination in China, migration throughout Central Asia by means of caravan routes, to its eventual appearance in Europe where it was introduced by the Moors during their conquests—is well documented elsewhere and not relevant to this discussion. It is sufficient to point out that, in the 2,000 years since its inception, paper making has remained unchanged in its basic principle. A dilute slurry of beaten (macerated) cellulose fibers is passed over a fine mesh screen. The pulpy fiber remains matted on the screen while the water drains through. The mat of fibers, once dry, holds together in what we recognize as a sheet of paper.

Raw Materials

The basic raw matter which is used to make paper, cellulose, is, to varying degrees, a structural element of all plants—some of which are very amenable to forming paper, others far less so. Flax (linen) and cotton have been the traditional European source, mainly because of the high proportion of cellulose which they contain and because of the durability of the individual fiber. But more than two-thirds of all paper made nowadays is composed entirely or partially of wood pulp. This is undesirable for fine art, as such paper tends to be too acidic, crumbling and yellowing with age. In addition, the fibers of wood pulp are short and relatively brittle, making the paper particularly unsuitable for the rigors of printmaking. Interestingly, some very fine Japanese papers contain a proportion

40. Microscopic structures of cellulose fibers in hand-formed sheets of paper

Japanese print paper (200x)

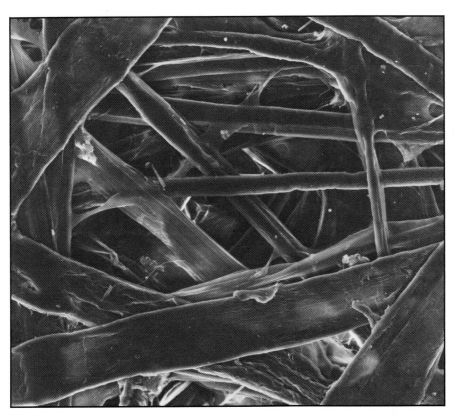

Japanese print paper (800x)

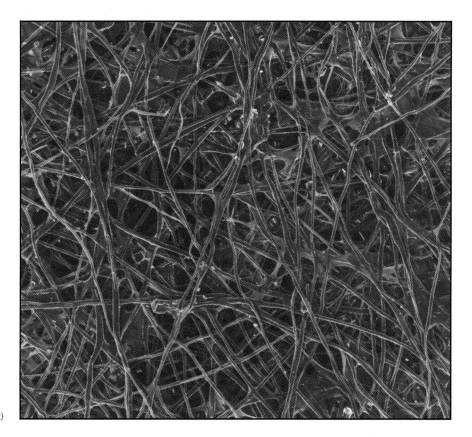

Indian print paper (200x)

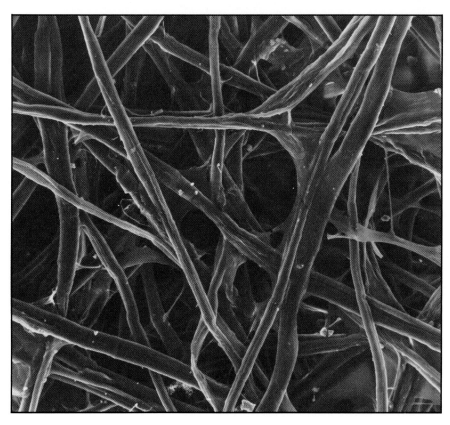

Indian print paper (800x)

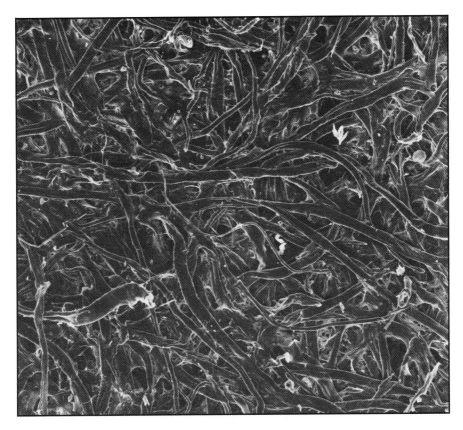

Arches cover (200x)

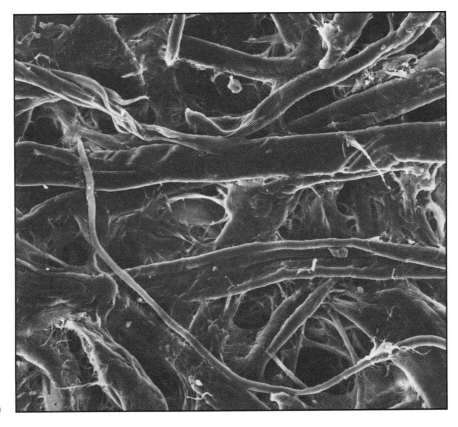

Arches cover (800x)

of wood pulp, which in no way seems to endanger longevity or strength. This is probably because there are no chemical additives in these papers, as there are in American wood pulp papers.

Some of the best hand-made papers come from Japan (although China and Korea also produce very fine papers), where the tough, rugged character of the fibers used make them exceptionally durable. It can be argued that the simple, almost ritualistic manner in which the paper is made, as well as the reverence in which it is held, are decisive factors in producing such exquisite results.

No matter what the source, whether vegetable, grass leaf or bark, all paper is affected by climate. Cellulose fibers have a strong affinity for water, and the paper (unless it has been somehow sealed) will always maintain the same humidity as the surrounding air.

To a large extent, the density and strength of paper are dependent on the amount of beating or pounding which its fibers have undergone. Consider two extremes: blotting paper and glassine. The former is lightly beaten and the fibers subsequently bond precariously while the latter has been beaten to such a degree that the paper is extremely hard, translucent and practically impermeable. In general, pounding the pulp with a mallet for paper produces a longer fibered, stronger paper than mechanical beating, which cuts and weakens the fibers.

Additives

Almost every kind of paper contains some form of additive, depending on the use for which the paper is intended, or the effect or color desired. Typical additives are fillers, size and coloring agents. Fillers are inorganic pigments which may be clay, chalk or titanium dioxide; they contribute opacity and a certain brightness, depending on which type has been used. Most papers are tinted, if not colored. The term "white" covers a wide range of nuances of shades from cool to yellowish warm.

The most common additive is sizing, which is either "internal" (introduced during beating or stock preparation) or "external" (individual sheets are coated once formed and dried); its purpose is to render the paper impermeable—whether partially or totally depends on the amount of and type of size. It also strengthens the paper. Rosin is the most common internal sizing agent. Its percentage range (given as a percentage of the weight of the paper) varies from 0.5% to 4.0%. Any paper containing more size than this is called "hard-sized."

Commonly used external sizing is starch—usually corn, potato, tapioca or sorghum—which does not have a great deal of effect on the paper's resistance to water and inks, but strengthen it and give it smoothness. Papers whose surfaces are required for printing upon will be coated with size to give additional strength. Etching requires a paper which contains a balanced amount of size—neither too little, which would leave the paper so weak that it would disintegrate when wet, nor too much, which would block the paper's absorption of ink into its pore structure. (Paper which contains no sizing whatsoever is called "waterleaf.")

Other materials are added to paper for visual effect. Coarsely-ground fibers such as dried corn stalk, onion skin or cattail may also be included with the basic pulp to give interesting structures, and subtle hints of natural color.

At present, paper is made three ways: machine made, by far the most common method, responsible for all commercial paper products; handmade, in which each sheet is formed individually and manually; mold made, which, although partially mechanized, simulates in certain respects the hand-made paper. Into the latter category fall such widely used printmaking papers as Arches Cover and Rives BFK. Complex machinery, while it is continuously being updated and made more efficient to facilitate higher rates of production, does not foster qualities desirable for printmaking paper. Due to the manner in which the machine operates, the fibers tend to flow in one direction, lengthwise, giving the paper a "grain." This weakens the paper across the breadth of the sheet. In this respect, the advantage of a hand-formed sheet of paper is that its fibers interlock securely length and breadth-wise, rendering the paper more stable and less susceptible to buckling and cockling. In other words, the sheet of paper is equally strong in all directions, as opposed to having directional weaknesses.

Production of commercial papers is completely mechanized and the most commonly employed machine is the Fourdrinier, which forms paper in a continuous roll, cuts it into sheets and dries the sheets at a high rate of output. Calendering may also be done as a final step. This hardens the surface of the paper and gives it a final sheen.

At the other end of the scale, very acceptable paper may be made with the simplest of equipment. A basin or a small vat, mold and deckle and a few felts (preferably wool, although other fabrics may be experimented with) are sufficient.

Lured by the thought of making their own papers, an increasing number of printmakers are trying this ancient skill for themselves. The involvement resulting from their fascination is a step toward drawing them into greater intimacy with the processes of printmaking and the innumerable ways in which they can combine the materials.

Behavior of Paper in Printmaking

To enhance our understanding of the paper and the plate as they merge within the press, we should ideally be able to observe what actually happens during this time. In lieu of this, we can try to visualize and become sensitive to their union.

Etching requires three qualities in paper: pliability, strength and the capacity to absorb ink. The first two are interrelated—the paper must endure tremendous pressure from the press and be resilient enough to be forced into deeply etched grooves and crevices without tearing or showing stress. Many acid-bitten areas in the plate which have not been scraped back or modified in any way are sharp edged. It takes a tough fiber and a well-formed sheet of paper to withstand being cut and torn.

How well a printmaking paper absorbs ink depends on how it is humidified before printing on it. Proper humidification improves the paper in three ways: (1) It causes the paper to swell in size, increasing the volume of the spaces between fibers and allowing it to absorb more ink; (2) It swells the fibers themselves, increasing their pliability; (3) It dissolves the excess size on the paper surface which would interfere with the absorption of ink.

The factor of surface texture is important in etching papers. The best of them have a rough surface, which further enhances their pliability and ink absorption.

In a good printing, 70% of all ink, whether surface or intaglio, ought to be transferred. It has already been pointed out that paper is most receptive when the fibers have had a chance to swell to their limit, rendering them as pliable as possible.

Dipping the paper in water for a few minutes and then squashing it between sheets of blotting paper will not produce the best, or even reasonably good results. Paper is best prepared at least a day before it is required to print. Held by diagonally opposite corners, one sheet is passed slowly through a bath of water, allowed a few seconds for excess water to drip off it, then laid gently inside a clean plastic bag. Once a pile of the required number has been built up, the plastic bag is sealed by folding the open ends under it. In this humid atmosphere, the paper absorbs the correct amount of moisture. By the time of printing, the paper should be cool to the touch but not damp. A large soft sponge should be used to remove excess moisture.

It is essential to take the time to reflect on these details (which are admittedly the less showy aspects of printmaking), since they make the print.

41. Diagram: Paper absorption of ink

Ink rolled

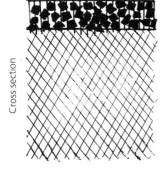

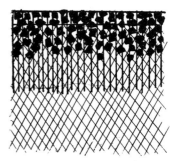

Cross section

Stages in ink penetration

B. Viscosity Processes in Color Printing

In the history of printmaking, as we have seen, artists have sought to simplify colors by integrating them simultaneously on one plate and printing the plate in a single pass through the press. At Atelier 17, many processes were tried, including offsetting, stenciling and combination methods, to achieve this end. Artists observed, however, that they could not superimpose color layers simultaneously in a consistent manner. They could not print in color predictably.

The discovery that raw linseed oil modifies the interaction of color layers has solved this problem, and has led to a new understanding of the color printmaking process. The use of raw linseed oil has made it possible to superimpose as many color layers as desired on a single plate. Moreover, raw linseed oil, by modifying the viscosity of color layers, creates an attraction between them.

When we superimpose two color layers we see that only their surface films interact. By wetting one of the inks with raw linseed oil we cause its surface film to be absorbed by the other drier ink. This absorption resembles a magnetic attraction. By making the wet ink wetter with more raw linseed oil, the absorption of the wet ink by the dry ink becomes greater. In addition, by rolling the ink with greater pressure, we cause more films of the wet layer to be absorbed by the dry layer. This understanding comes gradually with increasing experience in mixing and rolling colors. Combining this modification of inks by raw linseed oil, with an understanding of viscosity and tackiness of inks, aids in realizing clarity and richness of color in the prints. An edition of prints may also be produced in a more predictable way.

1. Color Viscosity: Its Nature and Behavior

Viscosity and the Interaction of Color Layers

In the earlier section on oils, we defined the properties of viscosity and tackiness in the polymer chains of a cooked linseed oil. Viscosity was defined as the inward pull developed by a polymer chain and its resulting resistance to flow; and tackiness, as the adhesive quality of the chain in sticking to other substances. When the ink is mixed well, the long polymers constituting it weave around each other and form three-dimensional meshworks with huge spaces between the chains.

We must now focus on the interaction of different layers of ink with each other. An ink made of long polymer-oil is a dry ink (called so because the oil has been cooked to dry); the polymers are viscous and hold themselves together in the manner of dry, flexible sticks. In an ink layer, they mesh together with very large spaces between them. When liquids like kerosene or raw linseed oil come into contact with a dry ink layer, the liquid molecules find their way in between the oil polymer chains, moving them apart and causing them to flow, reducing the viscosity of the ink.

When a dry ink layer is rolled over a layer of wet ink (wetted with raw linseed oil), the dry ink layer tends to absorb the wet ink as it did the liquids. One can call this absorption, a "sponge-like effect." It is by understanding this effect that we are finally able to superimpose or juxtapose colors in desired ways.

Tackiness (stickiness or adhesivity)

Tackiness is the binding quality or adhesive force developed by the ink in contact with other materials such as paper, metal, rollers, glass, etc. The more viscous an ink the tackier it is. Our concern throughout the printing process is to lay down a predictable amount of ink on the paper. Since at each stage we transfer the ink—from glass slab to roller to plate to paper—less and less of it reaches the next stage. At the final point a very small proportion of the original amount of ink is actually deposited on the paper; most of it still adhering to the plate, the rollers and the slab. The effective transfer of the ink is dependent on the tackiness.

Pure Raw Linseed Oil

Raw linseed oil is a free flowing liquid (like water or other solvents), made of small, free-moving molecules. It is this quality that makes it useful in changing the viscosity and tackiness of cooked linseed oil, which, made of long polymers, is sticky and resists flow. Previously we saw how raw linseed oil molecules enter the spaces between the long polymer chains of the cooked linseed oil, forcing them apart and causing them to flow. The use of raw linseed oil to modify the behavior of inks is pivotal in viscosity color printmaking. By understanding how these oils behave, we can predict their interaction in the processes of structuring colors on the plate.

2. Demonstrations: Color Structuring

Materials

Raw purified linseed oil	*Spatulas (flat-edged)*
Red and Blue offset inks (Rubine Red and	*Clean glass slab (milk white glass or plate*
Process Cyan)	*glass backed with white blotter paper)*

42. Glass-topped table for rolling out inks

Juxtaposition of Colors

- □ Lay a spoonful of each color on the glass slab.
- □ Add about 10 drops of raw linseed oil to the red color and thoroughly mix it with a clean spatula. Notice that the ink becomes wet and flowing. We will call it a "wet" red.
- □ Add only 3 drops of oil to the blue color and mix it thoroughly with another clean spatula. The ink mixes and spreads well, as its heavy viscosity is slightly reduced, but still remains quite viscous and tacky: we will call it a "dry" blue.
- □ Spread a small quantity of red ink in a line with the spatula. Roll out the line of color into a thin layer with a brayer. Repeat this with a blue ink. In this process each brayer carries a thin layer of color. The thickness of the color films can be easily observed by watching the transparency and the intensity of each color layer rolled out by the brayers on the glass slab.
- □ Roll the brayer coated with the wet red color on a clean area of the slab. Roll the brayer coated with the dry blue color across the patch of red color, going slightly beyond it.
- □ Observe that where the blue brayer rolled over the red color, the red seems untouched by the blue; but where the blue roller went beyond the red patch, the blue ink rolled onto the slab right next to the red. Thus the red and blue colors are juxtaposed on the slab.

Upon closer examination, we see that where the dry blue rolled over the wet red, the red layer is reduced in color intensity. If we examine the blue brayer we see that red ink has been picked up onto its surface. In fact, depending on its dryness, the blue brayer has picked up nearly half the layer of red ink, (we can see this clearly if we now roll the brayer on another area of the slab). The greater the difference in the viscosities of the inks, the more the wet color will be picked up by the dry color brayer.

105

Superimposition of Colors

The same materials are used for this demonstration as are used for the one on juxtaposition. Make sure to start with clean, dry brayers.

- ◻ Lay out the inks as for the juxtaposition demonstration.
- ◻ Reverse the viscosity of the inks this time. Add 3 drops of raw linseed oil to the red ink and 6 drops to the blue.
- ◻ Roll out thin layers of red and blue with different brayers.
- ◻ Roll out a layer of the dry red ink in a clean area of the slab. The brayer coated with the wet blue ink is rolled across the red going slightly beyond it.
- ◻ Observe that where the wet blue has been rolled across the dry red, the blue is superimposed on the red, turning it into a violet color. The wetter the blue ink is, the more of it is absorbed by the red. If we examine the blue brayer, we see that it has lost about half of its ink, but has not picked up any red ink.

Notice in this demonstration that the raw linseed oil in the wet color was twice as much as in the dry color—6 drops in blue as opposed to 3 drops in red. We may superimpose as many layers of color as we wish, if, to each teaspoonful of a new oncoming color we add 3 more drops of raw linseed oil (example: red 3 drops, blue 6 drops, yellow 9 drops, etc.)

In juxtaposition, however, we are limited in the number of layers of colors we can use. This is because the amount of oil that we must add to each successive layer doubles (example: red 3 drops, blue 10 drops, yellow 20 drops, etc). Very soon as we have to keep doubling the oil quantity of each oncoming color, the large quantity of raw linseed oil in the ink layers destroys their viscosity effect, and starts flowing, blurring the ink.

If we juxtapose and superimpose different color layers on a carefully prepared intaglio plate with many different depths and textures, we can obtain any desired structures of color combinations and tonal values.

8 Experiments in Viscosity Processes

I developed the following experiments as part of my seminars and lecture-demonstrations during the time I taught and worked at Atelier 17 in Paris. They were the outgrowth of some years of personal experimentation with simultaneous color printmaking, plus the inspiration and stimulus I got from working with many groups of artists, at the Atelier and other workshops.

At the time I first came to work at Atelier 17, I was fascinated by the variety of color printmaking being explored there. This inspired me to work in color. My experience as a sculptor, coupled with my interest in color, encouraged me to take new approaches to color printmaking. Each different image I worked on seemed to demand new ways and means of bringing it to a fuller expression. By being deeply involved with these images and trying to keep my mind as open as possible, I had many exhilarating experiences that resulted in the transformation of both the intaglio plates and the prints.

Each of the experiments in this chapter presents one basic aspect of the many possible ones in viscosity color printmaking. Each is intended only as a starting point, to lead eventually to other explorations; none is an end in itself. These experiments share a common characteristic: the intaglio color plate can be etched, carved and engraved in the same amount of time, and with the same simplicity, as the successive states of a plate for black and white intaglio printmaking. In experiment C which follows (printing a plate in the "pointillist manner"), we see the working of the plate brought to the highest simplicity, directness and immediacy of expression.

Working with these experiments, the reader may gain a deeper insight into simultaneous intaglio and surface color printmaking processes, and be encouraged to continue working on his own.

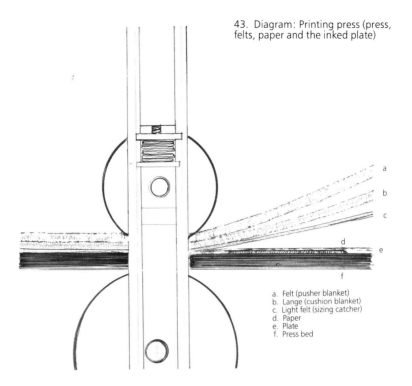

43. Diagram: Printing press (press, felts, paper and the inked plate)

a. Felt (pusher blanket)
b. Lange (cushion blanket)
c. Light felt (sizing catcher)
d. Paper
e. Plate
f. Press bed

Discussion

In this section we will take a relief plate, previously prepared—with its variety of levels of relief, textures, undulations, hard edges and aquatints—and apply colors to it, with rollers of different densities. We will print this plate in a single pass through the press. The possibilities of this process are extraordinary, both in the number and in the richness, vividness and intensity of colors achieved.

Printing by viscosity process is unique compared with other methods of printmaking, since it involves the simultaneous integration of intaglio and surface color. Because the quantities of the intaglio ink predominate in such prints, the character of the intaglio plate shows through. At the same time, we are faced with the challenge of balancing and integrating the heavy intaglio with the relatively thin layers of surface ink.

The intaglio plate always holds more ink in its crevices and deeply dug-out areas than on its surfaces, where the ink is rolled on thinly. Since intaglio ink contains 80% pigment, it will tend to dominate surface color, which has only 16% pigment. To knit together intaglio and surface colors, we can add transparent white ink to the intaglio, which reduces its pigment concentration and brings it close to the color intensity of the surface. Alternatively, we can increase the pigment density to emphasize local color in certain areas.

If the color intensity of surface inks is stronger than desired, it can be reduced in two ways: either we can thin down the layer of surface ink that we roll onto the plate, or we can add transparent white ink to surface ink, which reduces its color intensity without thinning the layer of ink. We can also "body" surface inks by adding more pigment to them to bring them closer to the color intensity of intaglios.

In trying to superimpose surface colors on the intaglios, we must consider the difference in viscosity between them. We must be aware that soft rollers have a tendency to pick up some intaglio ink as they penetrate the deeper surfaces of the plate.

Offset inks coming directly from a can have to be modified to create viscosity and color relationships. We use various substances for this purpose—raw linseed, magnesium carbonate, French chalk, Vaseline, pigments, etc. These substances must be added carefully, since too much of a modifier may overwhelm the properties of an ink.

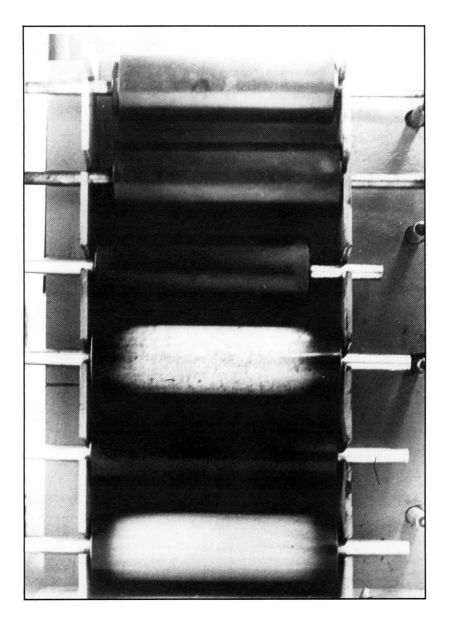

44. Roller stand with rollers of different densities

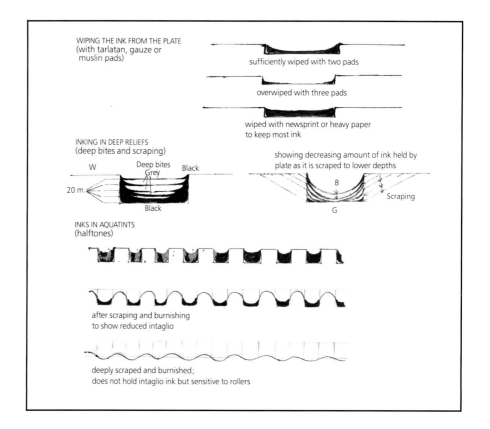

45. Diagram: Intaglio inking

WIPING THE INK FROM THE PLATE
(with tarlatan, gauze or muslin pads)

sufficiently wiped with two pads

overwiped with three pads

wiped with newsprint or heavy paper
to keep most ink

INKING IN DEEP RELIEFS
(deep bites and scraping)

W
Deep bites
Grey
Black

20 m.

Black

showing decreasing amount of ink held by
plate as it is scraped to lower depths

B

Scraping

G

INKS IN AQUATINTS
(halftones)

after scraping and burnishing
to show reduced intaglio

deeply scraped and burnished;
does not hold intaglio ink but sensitive to rollers

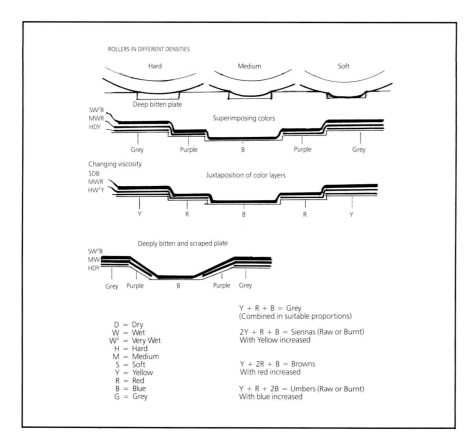

46. Diagram: Surface color rolling

ROLLERS IN DIFFERENT DENSITIES

Hard   Medium   Soft

Deep bitten plate

SW²B
MWR
HDY

Superimposing colors

Grey   Purple   B   Purple   Grey

Changing viscosity
SDB
MWR
HW²Y

Juxtaposition of color layers

Y   R   B   R   Y

Deeply bitten and scraped plate

SW²B
MW
HDY

Grey Purple   B   Purple Grey

D = Dry
W = Wet
W² = Very Wet
H = Hard
M = Medium
S = Soft
Y = Yellow
R = Red
B = Blue
G = Grey

Y + R + B = Grey
(Combined in suitable proportions)

2Y + R + B = Siennas (Raw or Burnt)
With Yellow increased

Y + 2R + B = Browns
With red increased

Y + R + 2B = Umbers (Raw or Burnt)
With blue increased

Preparation of the Intaglio Plate and the Inks

Plate Preparation

We begin fashioning an image from the plate sculpturally—by etching and/or carving, cutting, gauging and engraving. With one or all of these methods, we can create a plate in full relief, with a wide range of sculptural levels and textures. The plate made in this way becomes a landscape, a canyon land with different terraces, pinnacles, depths and rugged textures. The relief surfaces of the plate should be properly polished and burnished to remove fine scratches that would intaglio ink in unwanted places, influencing the rolled-on surface colors detrimentally. A variety of materials can be used for polishing—various grades of emery paper, fine steel wools, rouge or putz pomade, metal polishes, burnishers, etc.

Intaglio printmaking differs from the various methods of surface printing in that the maximum amount of ink must be pulled out of the deep crevices of the plate onto the paper. If the intaglio ink is excessiviely viscous or tacky, an insufficient quantity of it will be released onto the paper. To correct this, we must modify the ink with raw linseed oil and mix it thoroughly. If it is too flowing we can add a small amount of French chalk to thicken it. To enhance the color intensity of the ink we can mix into it some powdered pigment. Used sparingly, a touch of Vaseline will cut the tack of the ink. Thorough mixing is essential when using all of these additives. The plate should be warm while the ink is applied. This will release the ink more effectively to the paper during printing. Since the plate is in full relief, the paper should be sufficiently flexible to bend down into the deep crevices and various levels of the plate to pull out the most ink. Therefore it should be 100% rag, fairly thick and dampened to the proper humidity.

Offset Inks

Offset ink has a different composition and method of application than intaglio, consequently it is prepared differently. Offset ink has only 16% of pigment (the balance being cooked linseed oil), and is a more delicate ink than intaglio. Since offset is rolled in thin layers onto the surfaces of the plate, it is also less concentrated. Offset inks should be handled carefully to avoid muddying their colors. Modifiers must be added with more care to offset inks than to intaglio inks; offset inks are more susceptible to being overwhelmed by modifiers than are intaglios.

Color Ink Set-Up

A proper set-up is crucial to organize color printmaking. When properly organized one can pull a print with any desired number of colors in a matter of minutes. This approach preserves the freshness and spontaneity of printmaking. The most essential element of the set-up is a large table for rolling colors. The table top should be covered by large glass slabs at least 1/2" thick, either milk white or clear glass with white blotter paper underneath it. There should be enough area on the table to accommodate at least three rollers. The rollers are of three grades of firmness—hard, medium and soft. When not used they should be kept clean and smooth, with the roller surfaces not in contact with any other object. The rollers must only be cleaned with Kerosene, since any other solvent dissolves and destroys their surfaces.

Materials

A prepared zinc plate
Intaglio ink—Benzidine Yellow
Offset inks—Rubine Red, Process Cyan and
   Transparent White
Raw linseed oil (in a drip-spout condiment
   bottle)

Magnesium Carbonate and French chalk
Vaseline or White Petroleum Jelly
Spatulas (flat-edged), at least half a dozen
Rollers—hard, medium and soft
Etching paper (rag paper)
Tarletan

Experiment A.: Printing by juxtaposition of colors

First we lay out the colors. Yellow intaglio ink is put on a glass slab next to the hot plate. A quantity of each of transparent white, red and blue ink are set out on a color table (a table covered with plate glass). Compared to black intaglio inks, pigmented intaglios are usually more viscous and tacky. We can modify these properties by adding either additional powdered pigment or magnesium carbonate. A few drops of raw linseed oil are added to the ink, and it is mixed thoroughly with a spatula. A touch of Vaseline often helps cut the stickiness of the ink.

The three surface colors differ in viscosity—the blue ink will be dry, the red, medium wet, and the transparent white, very wet. Roughly 20 drops of linseed oil are added to each teaspoonful of the transparent white ink to make it *very wet and flowing*. A small dot of a tertiary color mixed from the red, yellow and blue inks can also be added to provide a subtle tone to the ink (the tone can vary from warm to cold). Add about 10 drops of raw linseed oil to each teaspoonful of the red ink and mix well. This ink should be *less wet* than the transparent white. Add only a couple of drops of raw linseed oil (to make the ink spread well) to each teaspoonful of the blue ink and mix well. Its heavy viscosity and tackiness are slightly reduced; this is the *dry* color. In this process the hard roller carries a thin layer of the very wet transparent white color, the medium roller carries a layer of medium-wet red ink, and the soft roller carries a layer of dry blue ink. Roll out and spread a thin layer of each color on the glass slabs with the appropriate roller.

◻ Lay the plate on the heat source. Rub Yellow intaglio ink into the plate with a small wad of tarletan (starch removed and smooth). Then wipe the plate with pads made of starch-free tarletan, the first pad spreading the ink and taking away most of the excess, and the second pad wiping surfaces clear of ink. Hand-wipe, as the final step, to fully clean unwanted ink from the plate surface.

◻ Roll the hard roller coated with the very wet transparent white color over the plate without applying any pressure.

◻ Follow with the medium roller using slight, steady pressure to reach the middle areas of the plate.

◻ Reinforce the transparent white by passing the hard roller over the plate a second time.

◻ Follow this by the soft roller covered with dry blue ink, with enough pressure to reach the deeper areas of the plate.

◻ Then place the plate on the bed of the press and print.

◻ The print will show a range of colors—the yellow intaglio, some areas of blue, some of red—juxtaposed with each other and with areas of transparent white.

If we reverse the viscosities of red and blue inks and repeat the process above, we will notice a different effect in the print. The red and blue inks will have mixed or super-imposed. Besides experimenting with the interaction of the surface colors it is important for us to experiment with changing the color of the intaglio. Darker colors tend to show the depths and textures of the plate.

Experiment B: Printing by superimposing colors

In this experiment, besides superimposing colors, we will also reverse the order of rollers, starting with the soft roller and ending with the hard. We will also build the colors by starting with the lightest color and build up to the darkest.

The intaglio for this experiment is a very light tertiary color. The soft roller takes a dry yellow ink, the medium roller a medium wet red, and the hard roller has a very wet blue. In superimposing colors, we normally wet each by mixing in only 3 more drops of raw linseed oil per teaspoon than the previous, drier color. For example, dry yellow, 3 drops; medium red, 6 drops; wet blue, 9 drops, and so on.

◻ Ink the plate with intaglio and wipe.

◻ Roll the soft roller with the dry yellow ink onto the plate, with enough pressure to reach the deeper layers of the plate.

◻ Roll the medium roller with the medium wet red onto the plate with moderate pressure. Where this ink contacts surfaces covered with yellow ink, the two superimpose to make orange.

□ The hard roller, with the wet blue, contacts only the top surface of the plate when it is rolled on without pressure. The top surfaces turn dark since yellow, red and blue are superimposed.

In the previous experiment the rollers will penetrate the plate to a certain depth only. The lowest depths will yield intaglios and ivory, whites depending on the degree of wiping. With the above superimposition experiment we see through transparent darks; the beauty of this method lies in the depths we can realize in the plate. There are, of course, an infinite number of different experiments that we can perform with these processes.

Experiment C: Printing in color in the "pointillist manner"

This is a highly advanced technique that was recently developed. The plate is prepared by creating textures and reliefs through the use of etching, engraving, aquatint, mezzotint, photo halftones, or carved and worked with hand or machine tools. It is then printed by the simultaneous process of structuring colors in points or streaks of color side by side—juxtaposed. This method, when fully developed and perfected, will bring about a tremendous change in printmaking as it simplifies technical processes while creating powerful and intense colorfields never before realizable.

□ Prepare a plate with a series of grades of aquatints, biting time in the acid ranging between 5 and 45 minutes, with 5 minutes between each exposure. (Described later on under "Developing a Plate for Exp. C.")

□ Lay two color on a glass slab (red and blue) and as in Experiment A, prepare a yellow intaglio.

□ Make the red wet with raw linseed oil.

□ Add a couple of drops of raw linseed oil to the blue to make it easier to spread, but still viscous and tacky.

□ Lay the plate on the hot plate and ink it with the yellow intaglio; wipe it properly and move it to a nearby slab.

□ With a soft roller and a steady vertical pressure, roll the blue color on the plate.

□ Print the plate.

The juxtaposition of small dots or spots of pure colors creates a color field with vibrant luminosity. As the colors blend in the eye, the fresh, shimmering effects create a new dimension in printmaking. We can also use the viscosity printing process, utilizing the variations in depth of an aquatinted plate which is in fact a miniature relief plate. (1) The yellow intaglio is in the deepest parts of the plate; (2) by rolling a hard roller with wet red, the red color is placed on top in dots (reds on the top surfaces of the aquatint); (3) a soft roller with dry blue color is rolled over the red; it lies in rings or streaks around the red dots and descends. (Since the soft roller has in the process picked up some of the red onto itself, the red remaining is different in quality than previously.) (4) The three colors are thus juxtaposed in tiny dots and streaks.

The color field these colors produce may be varied by controlling their relative amounts. With suitable proportions of the three colors, we can obtain silvery, transparent grays. With different depths of aquatints, the quantity of the intaglio yellow color can be increased or decreased to produce Siennas. Depending on the density of the incisions or the amount of the raised flat surfaces, we can increase the proportion of red to get various browns. By playing with the thickness of the blue films we can increase the intensity of blue to produce umbers. Through experiments such as these we have a chance to work with fresh possibilities and potentialities for expression.

Developing a Plate for Experiment C

Developing an image in full relief on a plate having different levels, we can build color prints that will include all the primaries, secondaries and tertiaries together on that one plate, opening up tremendous possibilities.

- Start with a plate in full relief.
- Scrape and burnish the hard edges of some of the relief levels to smooth or soften them, if desired.
- Lay a rough-grained aquatint all over the plate (bitten for 10 minutes).
- Lay another aquatint, fine-grained all over the plate (bitten for 10 minutes).
- Roll rough (350 to 400 grain) emery paper onto a sanding block and sand the entire plate. Sand the plate so that the aquatint recedes in depth where it approaches the top surfaces of the plate. The top surfaces are completely clear of aquatint.
- Using fine (600 grain) emery paper, fastened to the sanding block, sand the entire plate, reducing the top surfaces to a finer finish.
- Polish the surface of the plate to a high finish with crocus cloth mounted on the block.

We can also do the finishing steps above with a sander and the appropriate papers. At this stage, we may wish to do further work with scraper and burnisher selectively to remove texture and polish certain areas.

This prepared plate can now be used in the pointillist experiment or any other combinations of printing processes. The plate begins our discovery of a sensitive and powerful means of expression—one that is versatile and capable of infinite variations, that yields prints vibrantly shimmering with a full range of colors but that can be created as simply as an aquatint print in black and white.

Experiment D: Printing by separation of intaglio and surface color

In this process the plate is printed in two passes—once with all the rolled surface colors only, and once with intaglio only. The advantage of this process is that it prevents weakening of the intaglio color, especially in delicately worked plates (photo halftones and fine surface textures). In the viscosity process, (Experiments A, B and C) soft rollers charged with dry ink, as they are rolled with pressure over these plates, tend to pull the intaglio ink out of them. The print then shows a weakened intaglio. In addition, the amount of intaglio subtracted from each print is unpredictable. Printing intaglio and surface colors separately juxtaposes them better; they appear strong and sharp.

For this experiment a registration guide is prepared for the plate. The plate is laid face up in the center of a sheet of heavy printing paper and its outline traced. The size of the guide should be large enough to allow for a couple of inches of it to be locked under the roller of the press with the plate area clear of the roller. The paper on which we print should be the same size as the guide. The guide is then placed on the press bed.

- ☐ Prepare a relief plate with a series of deep open areas, textures and halftones.
- ☐ Layout and roll the surface colors for this experiment exactly as in Experiment A, except do not apply intaglio to the plate.
- ☐ Place the plate rolled with surface colors in the traced outline of the registration guide; lay the paper to be printed over them. After the first printing, make sure the press roller holds the end of the paper underneath it, lay the blankets and the print together back over the roller. To keep the paper humid, place a humidified blotter over it.

47. Diagram: Registering the plate
    (to print the plate in two passes)

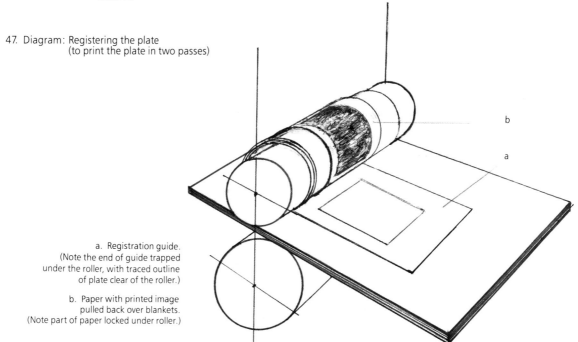

b

a

a. Registration guide.
(Note the end of guide trapped under the roller, with traced outline of plate clear of the roller.)

b. Paper with printed image pulled back over blankets.
(Note part of paper locked under roller.)

- Remove the plate, ink it with the intaglio color and wipe it properly. If the intaglio is a light color such as yellow, clean the plate before applying the intaglio.
- Replace the plate carefully in the traced outline of the guide. Roll back the paper and blankets onto the plate and print for the second time.

Sometimes the register is not absolutely accurate in this process since during the first printing the damp paper stretches in the direction of press travel. This off-register effect may add a quality of depth or three dimensionality to certain prints.

Experiment E: Printing without the use of viscosity

In this experiment we will use the aquantinted plate prepared for printing in color in the pointillist manner (Experiment C). This time, however, we will print the surface colors and the intaglio separately, as in Experiment D.

Preparation of Inks

Intaglio

Start by preparing a yellow intaglio ink. Since this ink is more viscous and tacky than is desirable, add to it a few drops of raw linseed oil and a touch of Vaseline.

Surface Colors

Lay a teaspoonful of each surface ink (red and blue) on a glass slab. Add a few drops of raw linseed oil and a touch of Vaseline to the red ink to make it spread well. Also add a few drops of linseed oil to the blue ink.
- With the medium roller, roll and spread a layer of red ink on the slab.
- With the hard roller, roll and spread a layer of blue ink on the slab.
- Roll the medium roller with the red ink over the plate, with enough pressure to reach the areas of relief.
- Using pieces of heavy paper (such as Arches paper or even pieces from old prints) and the flat of the hand, wipe the red ink off the surface of the plate. In the process of wiping, the ink settles around the edges of the deep reliefs and the areas of texture. Do not use tarletan or soft tissue for this wiping since they will wipe off too much of the ink at the edges of the reliefs and force it into the deep crevices intended for intaglio ink.

- Using the hard roller, roll the blue ink onto the plate without applying any pressure. The blue ink will only hit the top surfaces of the plate. The red and blue are juxtaposed, with the red forming rings, streaks or broken color areas around the blue relief areas.
- As in Experiment D, use a registration guide for the plate and the paper. Print the plate, take it off the press, and clean off any remaining surface colors (if the intaglio ink is dark, it is not necessary to clean the plate). The paper and guide remain locked under the press roller.
- Then ink the plate with the yellow intaglio color and wipe properly.
- Place the plate on the guide in the press and print for the second time.

In the final print we see the full effect of the color juxtaposition. The colors are sharp, strong and precise. For further experimentation, we could use more rollers or structure the colors in different combinations.

9 Simultaneous Color Printmaking by Combination Processes

The struggle to pull colors together onto one plate has continued all through this century. Artists have developed and tried various techniques of structuring many colors simultaneously on the same plate, both with intaglio and on the surface of the plate. In the technological atmosphere of the contemporary world, surrounded by a bewildering variety of materials and complex techniques, the artist is often compelled to elaborate on existing techniques, or bring new ones into play. At the same time, it is essential for the artist to seek unity and clarity in expressing his vision; to do this he must make sense of and simplify the means of achieving his desired result. With all the techniques available to him the artist may fall into the habit of gadgeteering; but guided by the vision of his image and his desire to simplify its expression, he will steer clear of this pitfall.

In addition to superimposing colors simultaneously on a single plate and printing colors in a pointillist manner, we can gain experience in other ways of bringing colors together simultaneously on the same plate, like that of printing by the ''a la poupée'' method, offsetting colors from other textures and images, stencilling or the contact processes.

It might seem that we are exaggerating or complicating our techniques; in reality we are absorbing or integrating other areas of printmaking to enrich the processes of building the image.

Materials

An intaglio plate in relief, with a variety of surfaces and textures

Various textured surfaces of cloth, wood, metal, torn or crumpled paper, etc.

Collages of different textures

Collagraphs

Wax paper

Prepared lino or wood cuts

Offset inks—Rubine Red, Process Cyan, Benzidine Yellow, Transparent White and Black

Intaglio inks (Blue-Black and Transparent White)

Raw linseed oil (in a drip-spout condiment bottle)

Magnesium Carbonate and French Chalk

Vaseline or White Petroleum Jelly

Spatulas (flat-edged)—at least half a dozen

Brayers (2'' diameter x 6'' length) and a medium hand roller

Etching paper

Tarletan (prepared)

1. Offset Processes

We can superimpose several colors simultaneously onto the surface of an intaglio plate by transferring them from various textured or worked surfaces. This not only provides color to the print but also enriches it by adding greater strength and structure to the intaglio composition. Depending on the needs of the plate, we can transfer to it different colors from various textured surfaces, collages, collagraphs, linoleum and wood blocks or photographic plates.

a) Offsetting Colors from Textures, Collages or Wood and Lino Blocks onto the Intaglio Plate

This process involves preparation of two different surfaces or collages, each for a different color. Colors are picked up from their surfaces simultaneously upon a clean roller and rolled on the surface of a plate with intaglio color.

- □ Ink the intaglio plate in brown color and wipe.
- □ Ink one textured surface (or Collage) in yellow, the other in blue, with brayers.
- □ Roll a clean roller over each inked texture or collage to pick up each separately.
- □ Now roll (offset) the two rollers with the offset textures or collages onto the intaglio plate, one over the other.

b) Offsetting Colors from Wood and Lino Blocks onto the Intaglio Plate

In this process we superimpose two relief images, each in a different color, onto the surface of an intaglio plate. The linoleum blocks are worked to coordinate with the image in the intaglio plate, to superimpose and structure their colors properly on it.

- ☐ Ink the intaglio plate in blue and wipe.
- ☐ Ink both linoleum blocks, one in yellow and one in red.
- ☐ Set the intaglio plate and the two linoleum blocks in a line on the glass slab, spaced so that a roller, passing over the lino blocks and onto the intaglio plate, superimposes the second lino image on top of the first and both of them onto the intaglio plate. Mark the positions of the intaglio plate and the first and second lino blocks carefully and accurately on the glass slab. To successfully transfer the second lino image onto the first, the ink on the second lino block should be wetter than that on the first lino block.
- ☐ With a clean roller (4″ or more in diameter), roll across the first and second lino blocks and onto the intaglio plate. Be careful not to pick up or slide the roller during its travel. The two lino images are superimposed one on top of the other and on the surface of the plate.
- ☐ Re-ink the plate and place back in its markings on the glass slab. Re-ink the first and second lino blocks, but do not remove from their places. Clean the roller that offsets the images before each offsetting.

2. Stenciling Methods

To superimpose a number of colors simultaneously on a single plate with the aid of stencils, we have to give the utmost attention to the viscosity of each of the colors so that we can control this process. The advantage of stencils is that we can print the plate with many superimposed colors in one operation without the problems of registration. As each of these stenciled color areas on the plate is flat and hard-edged, how they dominate the color scheme of the entire intaglio plate must be taken into consideration in planning the composition and building the plate.

Preparation of the Stencil

Any kind of strong and slightly thick paper—wax paper or ink resistant paper—can be used for making the stencil. This material should be slightly larger than the intaglio plate.

Ink the plate with black intaglio ink and wipe. Pull a print on a piece of stencil paper (not dampened) and give time to dry. Prepare several black and white prints this way on stencil paper. When the prints are dry, cut the openings for applying colors in the scheme needed. Use a sharp knife or razor blade to cut the openings in the stencil. When starting out, the artist might use one stencil for each color.

Use gelatin brayers or soft rubber rollers to roll out thin, even films of color through the stencil onto the plate. Several colors can be applied using one stencil if the color areas are far apart.

Several separate stencils can be used to superimpose a series of colors, where the stencil openings overlap. The first stenciled color layer applied to the plate should be the driest; each successive color layer should be a little wetter than the previous one. To repeat prints properly, the thickness of the color layers on the rollers should be maintained.

Prepare an intaglio plate as described in previous sections. Also prepare three stencils, one for each color, so that the openings in all three stencils overlap each other somewhat.

- Mix a violet intaglio ink, with a touch of black.
- Prepare the three surface colors—yellow, red and green—separately on the glass slab; roll out a thin layer of each using brayers. Make the yellow the driest of the three colors and the green the wettest. The difference in wetness between the colors should be no more than a few drops of linseed oil.
- Apply the intaglio ink to the plate and wipe it.
- Lay the first stencil on the plate and roll the yellow ink through the stencil on the plate.
- Repeat, using second and third stencils for red and green respectively.

Where the stencils' openings overlap the same areas of the plate, the print shows the full superimposition of the three surface colors and the intaglio.

3. Contact Processes

The contact process involves taking an intaglio plate in full relief, placing it face down on a layer of ink rolled out on a slab and pounding the back of the plate. The beauty of the contact process lies in its heightening the expressive powers of the plate by the surface color that it gathers. Depending on how thickly the ink is rolled out on the slab, we can augment the intensity of the surface color. If a thin layer of color is rolled out, the plate gathers only a thin film of color; if a thick layer of color is rolled out it explodes in all directions on the plate surface. The expressive possibilities of the contact process are immediately apparent.

To print with predictable results, the plate preparation is of utmost importance. The contact process is more successful with plates worked in full relief. If the plate's surface is flat, in spite of proper contact, the colors might not settle properly. Also we have to take into account the dimensions of the different rolled areas in relation to the intaglio plate and the relative viscosity of the inks.

- □ Prepare an intaglio plate with a series of reliefs, textures and tones.
- □ Roll out a layer of ink on a glass slab.
- □ Turn the intaglio plate upside down and lay it right on the rolled color layer on the glass slab. Using your palm, uniformly beat the plate from the back. The plate is now ready for printing. Sometimes the plate is marked on the back side and beat it only on that spot each time. In this way, the contact of the plate can be limited only to that area.
- □ A series of contacts can also be superimposed in the same manner by varying the dimensions of the rolled areas on the glass slab and also the thickness of color films.
- □ For the intaglio plate to pick up the series of colors from the glass slab the viscosity of the inks, as well as the consistent impact of our palms while beating the plate, should be considered.

10 Other Color Printmaking Techniques

The traditional methods of color printmaking, such as multiple plates and "a la poupée," have remained largely unchanged. Since they are geared to large editions, these techniques must be predictable and faithfully exact every time to the original they are reproducing. Therefore they have become complex and full of difficulties. The three-color process, for example, uses one plate to print each of the three primaries; where the primaries superimpose, they produce compound tones. This requires mechanization and the services of experts. Predictability and mass production emphasize the product, and product-emphasis demands a technician/master printer.

There are artists, however, who are interested in experimenting with these processes without being controlled by them. In the spirit of play, they preserve an open mind and try combinations of any methods that they come across, in the hope that their images will derive strength from such methods. Contemporary experiments in this line have included intaglio combined with silkscreen, lithography, collagraphy and other processes.

As compared with other methods of color printmaking (lithography, silk screen, relief, etc.), color intaglio holds the promise of building colors in quantity as well as intensity. In a color intaglio plate, the color intensities vary according to the different depths worked in the plate, and how much ink they contain. All color methods based on an intaglio plate share this rich potential.

There are problems in this approach, however. Since heavy layers of ink are deposited on the paper by the printing of each intaglio plate, the print will smudge if one intaglio plate is printed immediately after another (wet on wet). So multiple plate prints should be dried carefully between the printing of each plate. If this is done, there is the further problem of the print stretching after each intaglio impression and throwing off the register between them. These problems are common to multiple plate intaglio, a la poupée and combinations of intaglio with lithography, silk screen, collagraphy and Chine Collé.

1. From Multiple Intaglio Plates

Materials

4 zinc etching plates, 9''x 12''
Intaglio inks—Rubine Red, Benzidine Yel-
  low, Blue and Black
Raw linseed oil
Etching paper (Arches or Rives B.F.K.)

Flat-edged flexible spatulas—at least half a
  dozen
Prepared tarletan
Magnesium Carbonate and French chalk
Vaseline or White Petroleum Jelly

Preparation

- Prepare the key plate first (the key plate contains the complete design and it is usually printed in black). Work the design as required using various acid methods and hand or machine tools. From this key plate, transfer the design to the other plates and work them as required.
- Prepare some black ink and ink up and wipe the key plate properly.
- Pull a print from the key plate.
- Transfer the design from the wet print onto a blank zinc plate, by running them together through the press. Then let the ink dry slightly on the plate before exposing it to the acid. This step is repeated for each color plate.
- Immerse the color plates for a minute or two in diluted nitric acid and rinse them off. Wherever the ink has not covered the plates, they will give an oxidized image of the design.
- Now work each color plate as needed to provide colors—primary or secondary—to the design. The plates can be designed in aquatints and textures to provide the predictable color or color mixture to each area of the print.
- Once the plates are satisfactorily prepared, lay out the primary colors and the black ink in separate areas on the glass slab. Add sufficient raw linseed oil into each ink and mix thoroughly so that it spreads well. If the ink is too flowing, mix some magnesium carbonate or French chalk into it. The tackiness of the ink can be cut by mixing in a touch of Vaseline.

□ Prepare the registration guide and printing paper as described in Chapter 8, under Experiment D. Lay the registration guide on the press bed.

Printing

We ink up each color plate with its intended color and wipe it properly. First print the yellow plate and then the other two color plates, and the key plate last of all. Each plate is carefully registered within the lines on the registration guide. This is exactly the same approach as in Experiment D of Chapter 8.

In printing plates with heavy intaglios, we should bear in the mind the caution given at the beginning of this chapter. Also the printing of large editions obliges us to change our working strategy somewhat. In large editions the plates and printing paper are registered precisely by a system of drilled pinholes, and each print is printed from only one plate at a time (for example, all of the prints are first run with only the yellow plate) and dried between printings.

2. By ''A La Poupée'' Intaglio Methods

''A la poupée'' is a simpler process than multiple plate printing since we are dealing with fewer plates to which we can apply many colors. There is also the possibility of starting with secondary and tertiary color mixtures to give local color effects akin to those in painting. We can combine ''a la poupée'' methods with multiple plates to augment the strength and intensity of colors in building the image.

Materials

Same as those mentioned under the description of multiple intaglio plates above, plus a number of rolled up strips of felt or fabric (''poupées'' or ''dollies'') for the application of different colors of ink.

Preparation

We prepare the key plate and two other plates (for color) for multiple intaglio plate printing.

The considerations of planning the placement of colors are different, however. The artist has the option of letting the key plate contain one or two colors besides black—

now work the color plates with textures and aquatint so each contains several colors applied "a la poupée." There is the possibility of applying a local secondary or tertiary color mixture or having two or more plates superimpose wet-on-wet to form secondary or tertiaries. (This is not always successful since thick layers of color tend to become muddy when mixed wet-on-wet, especially when they are applied to the paper from deeply bitten plates. But these difficulties can be overcome by repeated trials and experiments.)

Printmaking

- □ Using the multiple plate registration method, first print the color plates and then the key plate.
- □ In large editions, all of the prints with one plate may be printed at a time and dried before printing the next plate.

3. Intaglio with Lithographic Plates

By entering other terrains such as lithography, collagraphy and photo processes and combining them with intaglio, we are enriching color printmaking through our exploration of new materials and methods, bringing the medium closer to the artist. In lithography we use offet colors to ink the surface. Offset colors are more transparent and brilliant compared to intaglio colors. Intaglio colors, worked in the depths of the plate, are darker and more opaque.

Printing the intaglio and litho plates together we can obtain vibrant colors and interesting color combinations in the print.

In printing the plates, the exact methods practiced in the multiple-plate process are followed except that the three color intaglio plates are replaced with three lithographic plates.

Materials

Intaglio materials are the same as above, except only one zinc plate is used
Litho offset colors (Process Yellow, Rubine Red, Process Cyan and Black)

Three lithographic (aluminum) plates (same size as key plate)
Lithographic materials to prepare and print the plates

Prepare the key intaglio plate with a design (as described in the earlier chapter). Transfer the design to the three aluminum plates, using the methods described under the multiple-plate printing section; they are developed using litho processes. Prepare some intaglio ink for the key plate and lithographic inks for the aluminum plates separately.

Ink the key intaglio plate and the three litho plates separately, the litho plates using litho process. Use the multiple plate registration method to print the plates. First print the color litho plates, then the key plate. Printing the intaglio plate last will keep the reliefs and textures of the plate intact.

4. Intaglio with Screen Printing

The combination of silkscreen with intaglio first developed at Atelier 17, as a result of the efforts of Hayter and his colleagues to bring together many different colors simultaneously on a single plate. This process affords the advantage of developing a silkscreen image in conjunction with the intaglio plate with less time and effort than juxtaposing two intaglio plates (key and color plate). Silkscreen offers a bold simplification of color, yet at the same time the screen can support a detailed and complex image. The silkscreen can be made to function merely as a stencil or can contain delicate halftone fields of color.

Materials

The materials are the same as used in multiple plate intaglio with the following exceptions:

1 zinc plate is used instead of 4	*Silkscreen materials to make and print 1*
Silkscreen inks	*screen*

Preparation

Prepare the design on the intaglio plate. Transfer the design to the screen (before stretching it) indirectly by using a tracing of the intaglio image or directly by running the screen fabric and the lightly-inked plate through the press; back the screen with paper to protect press felts. Then stretch the screen and varnish in the areas to be blocked.

The intaglio ink is prepared as in previous sections. Prepare a silkscreen ink with a heavy, syrupy consistency. If it is too stiff, it can be thinned with a small amount of silkscreen mixing varnish. The silkscreen ink may be used opaque or may be prepared to be transparent. Opaque silkscreen ink stands out well in areas of the plate that hold less (or have been wiped clear of) intaglio ink. Transparent silkscreen ink works well with thin layers of intaglio ink.

Printmaking

- □ Prepare and wipe the intaglio plate in black or another color.
- □ Place the screen in correct alignment with the intaglio image underneath; squeeze the ink mixture through the screen stencil onto the plate directly, using evenly distributed pressure on the squeegee.
- □ Print the plate.

It may be difficult to superimpose two or more colors onto the intaglio plate through screen stencils because of both fouling and the risk of developing too heavy an ink layer. It is possible, with careful handling. The surface colors, being above the intaglio in the plate will, of course, appear underneath it.

Besides combining serigraphy and intaglio, we can also adopt photo-processes, collagraphy, chine collé and other methods for use with intaglio. This way we are enriching color printmaking and our experiments broaden our experience.

11 Problems in Color Printmaking

To pull crisp impressions with sharp colors and to produce multiple prints of high quality and precision, it is essential to have, first of all, a properly organized workshop with every material at hand and all equipment in working order. Also necessary are a good understanding of the materials and the equipment being used—their physical and chemical nature included—as well as of the interactions of one material with another. We need to be highly sensitive and aware in dealing with all the materials involved—such as wiping the plate, maintaining the viscosity and the thickness of the films of color that are rolled onto the plate and in sending the plate through the press for printing.

After meeting these conditions it is possible to understand the causes of problems that arise in the processes of printing, to correct these mistakes and solve the problems. The most common problems that arise in color printing are discussed below.

1. Maintaining Viscosity of Inks

The two most important factors in achieving the desired combination of colors in a sharply defined print are the maintainance of viscosity and the varying thicknesses of the films of ink. In spite of our understanding of the inks—the pigments combined with varnish, and the oils with which we control the viscosity, etc.—problems may arise in the course of printing and the relationship between the colors may be ruined.

□ Materials like kerosene and other solvents mix with the inks and ruin them. As these solvents are constantly being used for cleaning the rollers and the slabs on which we roll colors, they may come into contact with inks.

- Colors are normally rolled in thin layers. If the layers are excessively charged and superimposed, the thick films of ink may overwhelm each other and turn muddy.
- If the plate is kept too warm, the color layers, when rolled, easily begin to run and flow (as the colors when heated soften and begin to flow and lose their viscosity).
- If excessive pressure is applied on the roller handles while superimposing the colors on the plate, ink layers are forced together and may become muddy.

2. Controlling Tackiness of Inks

Tackiness is the measure of the stickiness of the ink. It is the adhesive force or the binding quality of the ink with other materials like paper, plates, rollers, glass slabs, etc. and most importantly, the adherence of one film of color to another. Tackiness in the ink is partly due to the viscosity of the heavy varnish in the inks and partly to the presence of synthetic resins. Tack is necessary in the ink if the sharpness of the image is to be retained when the ink is rolled . But excessive tackiness can cause printing problems.

   If the ink is too tacky, very little of it is transferred to the paper from the plate. The ink does not spread evenly on the glass slab. To solve these problems without affecting the viscosity of the ink too much we may:
- Add a few drops of linseed oil (along with a small quantity of magnesium carbonate to maintain the stiffness of the ink) and mixing thoroughly.
- Add a small quantity of an extender, tint base or transparent white plus a few drops of uncooked linseed oil. (This might, however, diminish the intensity of the color).
- Mix the color thoroughly with a spatula by adding a few drops of linseed oil, to loosen and reduce the tackiness of the ink.
- Adding a small quantity of a lower number of stand oil gives a honey-like quality to the color, with less tackiness. Because this oil contains shorter molecules and is less viscous, the color becomes more translucent but less intense.
- Add a non-fat, waxy compound or Petroleum jelly (Vaseline) or a few drops of reducing oil to reduce tackiness of the ink.

3. Scumming of Inks

In trying to superimpose one layer of color over another, sometimes a scum of greasy smudges of inks gather over the entire surface of the intaglio plate. This condition results from minute particles separating and becoming dissolved in the lower layers of wet, greasy color films. This tinted ink scum appears granulated and broken into dots. By proper understanding of this problem we can prevent scumming.

The following conditions may cause scumming:

- When the viscosities of two superimposed inks are too close to one another. This must be adjusted—by adding a few drops of pure, raw linseed oil to decrease the viscosity of one, and stiffening the other, by adding a heavier, cooked linseed oil and sometimes a touch of magnesium carbonate.
- If, in the juxtaposition of colors with rollers on the plate, the wettest color film is excessively wet, greasy, or too thick.
- Using excessive pressure while rolling the color on the plate.
- Having too thin or too thick layers of color films while superimposing colors—dirty and heavily-charged ink rollers, particularly when they carry greasy inks.
- Being careless, hesitant or abrasive while rolling of colors on the plate or stopping abruptly in the middle of rolling colors.
- Using inks made of dyestuffs that bleed, especially the transparent lakes. By adding a pinch of magnesium carbonate, the excessive dye is absorbed.
- Adding too much modifier (or too many modifiers) to the ink upsets the ink's balance.
- Rolling colors while the plate is still too warm.
- Printing in warm or hot weather.
- Allowing kerosene (used for cleaning) to seep into the colors through negligence.
- Not cleaning the plate properly.
- Using a plate that has rough or coarse surfaces.

4. Bleeding or Running of Intaglio and Offset Inks

When the inks bleed, the image becomes blurred. Both the intaglio and offset inks could bleed or run when too soft, oily inks, full of grease and containing a high percentage of fatty acid particles, are used—these inks lack the necessary body to hold together. The inks could bleed into the surrounding colors or seep through the paper when printed. So one should evaluate the viscosity and tackiness of these inks carefully and with the help of modifying agents, make them heavier in body.

- Overly greasy or wet ink causes bleeding. This can be modified with the addition of magnesium carbonate to the ink and a stiffer varnish, which makes the ink tackier and more viscous.
- Heat causes bleeding of colors on the plate as it loosens the polymers and makes the ink flow.
- Inks such as lakes that are made of dyestuffs tend to bleed. By adding a carrier or extender like magnesium carbonate or calcium carbonate (especially for intaglios), this condition can be modified.

Glossary

Printmaking Processes

A la poupée. A color printmaking process in which the intaglio plate is inked in different colors in different areas with "dollies" or "poupées" of rolled canvas or felt, and wiped one area at a time with tarletan and by hand. A gradation of tints or juxtaposition of different colors can be built simultaneously on the same plate by this process.

Aquatint. A technique for building tonal structures in an etching plate. The plate is evenly covered with a porous ground; all plate areas not to be treated tonally are stopped-out with hard ground. The plate is then exposed to a weak acid solution. This creates an even texture of closely-spaced pits in the tonal areas of the plate. How long the plate has been exposed to acid limits the depths of the pits, which in turn limits the amount of ink they hold and thus the tone they convey to the final print.

Chine Collé. An intaglio or lithographic process in which lightweight colored paper is glued to the etching paper and passed through the press simultaneously with the inked intaglio plate or litho stone.

Collagraphy. A printmaking process in which a relief plate is "built-up" of thin pieces of plastic, tissue or cardboard, or frequently thin textured mats glued together. This built-up plate is made waterproof with acrylic spray and prints are pulled from it.

Color Separation. In color printmaking, the preparation of a separate plate for each color to be printed in intaglio, woodcut or lithography.

Combination Processes. 1) In intaglio plate preparation, the working of a given plate with any combination of hand or machine tools and/or the various acid methods (line and open bite, soft ground, aquatint, etc.); 2) In printing, the combination of the intaglio plate image with textures and images produced by woodblock, litho, silkscreen, etc.

Crayon Manner. 1) Traditionally, an etching method that imitates the textures of chalk drawings. The intaglio plate is covered with etching ground and then worked with etching needles, roulettes and other instruments to give a chalk-like effect. After etching, the plate is often worked directly with the same instruments to augment the effect; 2) The same texture as above produced by drawing directly with crayon or pencil on the clean plate and then biting it in acid. One can also work directly with crayon or pencil on an aquatinted plate.

Deep Etch. The deep-biting in acid of an area of intaglio plate.

Drypoint. An intaglio technique in which the surface of the plate is cut and scratched with a very sharp steel point. The drypoint incisions leave an ink-holding "burr" that gives a tonal quality to the lines of a drypoint print.

Embossed Print. (Also inkless intaglio or blind embossing.) A print pulled from an intaglio relief plate with slightly raised surfaces created by etching, gouging, engraving and/or carving. The plate is run through the press without ink. The inkless image—that is, just the image created by the relief of the plate—is then transferred, or "embossed" onto the printing paper.

Engraving. The direct cutting of a surface of a plate with a graver or burin. The plate, which is usually metal but could be made of any hard material, is then inked and printed.

Etching. An intaglio process in which an etching needle is used to draw an image on a plate covered with acid resistant ground. Afterwards, the plate is bitten in an acid bath, creating incisions in which ink will later be retained and then transferred onto paper in the printing process.

Halftone. Any tonal area in an intaglio plate. There are several ways of building halftones on plates by aquatint and photo-halftone processes or by directly working with hand tools and machine tools. By working the depths of halftones, any tonal gradation from light to dark may be produced.

Intaglio. A printing process using an image formed of engraved, carved or acid-bitten lines or areas beneath the surface of a metal plate. These cavities are filled with ink and a print is pulled by contacting the plate and a sheet of damp paper under heavy pressure.

Lift Ground (Sugar Lift). An intaglio platemaking process that, like etching or engraving, gives a direct, autographic impression of the strokes forming an image. The image is drawn on the plate with a brush dipped in a water soluble, saturated sugar solution. Upon drying, the plate is covered with hard ground (which is also allowed to dry) and then immersed in water. All the ground covering the sugar solution areas flakes off the plate and exposes the bare metal. The plate is then either aquatinted and etched or deep-bitten directly. A recommended sugar solution is India ink mixed with saturated sugar solution, plus a touch of soft soap.

Lithography. A printing process in which an image is applied to a smooth stone (i.e. limestone) or an aluminum plate with a grease pencil, crayon or brush. The image is fixed with nitric acid and gum arabic and then wiped with water prior to being inked. The ink settles in the greased areas, while the wet, non-greasy areas will repel the greasy ink. The print is pulled in a special press.

Mezzotint. A plate-making process in which a metal plate with a dense, ink-holding texture is prepared by the artist with rocker or roulette and worked with a scraper and burnisher so that selected areas will print with medium or light tone. Mezzotint plates can produce prints with many tones, from velvety darks to sparkling lights.

Monotype. A printing process which gives one unique print. An image is drawn or painted on a blank (unbitten) plate of metal or plastic that is then passed through the press with a sheet of damp printing paper.

Offset. A commercial printing process which transfers an inked image to a rubber cylinder on an offset press, then to a paper. In combination with intaglio printmaking, the offset of an inked relief image, linocut, woodcut, photo image, collage or texture, onto an inked intaglio plate by means of a clean roller.

Open Bite. The etching of open areas (without any texture or aquatint) in an intaglio plate. All other areas of the plate are stopped-out with varnish. Further depths can be bitten in successive exposures to acid. How various open-bite areas of a plate print depends on how deep they are and how they were wiped after inking-up.

Photo-printmaking (photogravure). The process of producing a photographic image using lines, textures and halftones on a pre-photosensitized intaglio plate.

Rainbow Roll. A printing method in which an inking roller is simultaneously inked with bands of different colors and then applied to a surface to achieve a rainbow effect. Applied as an offset to intaglio, litho, silkscreen, etc.

Relief Printmaking. A printmaking process using the inked surface of a carved or gouged wood block or metal plate. Customarily, ink is rolled onto the printing surface with a firm roller and printed. The gouged depressions show as white uninked areas in the final print. Woodcut, wood engraving and surface intaglio are examples of relief printing.

Serigraphy (screen printmaking). A printing process in which ink is forced through a cloth stencil (a stretched screen made of porous fabric such as nylon whose non-image areas are covered with varnish) onto a paper or canvas.

Soft Ground Etching. A platemaking technique for transferring textures of materials such as lace, gauze, crinkled paper, etc. to an etching plate. The plate is covered with a special soft ground (made of hard ground and grease or petroleum jelly), which never dries completely and thus can be removed by scratching or pressure. The plate is laid ground side up on the press bed, covered with textural material as desired and a sheet of wax paper (to protect the press blankets), and run through the press. The wax paper is gently removed. When the material is peeled off, the ground is selectively peeled off with it, leaving textural patterns open to the action of the acid.

Stipple Engraving. A process in which tone is achieved through dots and short strokes produced by a burin. Darker tones are produced by increasing the density of dots on the plate.

Tone Processes. Printmaking methods which yield tonal, as opposed to linear, surfaces. Tones can be created by aquatinting, photo processes, hand and machine tools, etc.

Wood Cut. A relief printing process that produces a carved and gouged side-grain wood block for pulling prints. Paper is placed over the inked surface areas and the image transferred to the paper by rubbing the paper against the block with a spoon or by passing block and paper through a press.

Wood Engraving. A relief printmaking process similar to wood cut, but done with engraving tools and producing an end-grain woodblock. Because of the grain closeness and lack of bias in end-grain wood, wood engraving tools cut freely in any direction on it, and can create extremely fine lines and textures. A wood engraving is printed in the same way as a wood cut.

Materials

Acid. A corrosive agent used to bite intaglio plates. The most frequently used acids are nitric acid, Dutch mordant (hydrochloric acid and potassium chlorate), and ferric chloride. Concentrated nitric acid has a tendency to "underbite" (bite sideways) while biting downwards in the plate. Diluted nitric acid and the other acids are more predictable in their effect on the plate.

Arkansas Stone. A stone used to sharpen etching and engraving tools such as burins, gouges, scrapers, needles, etc.

Asphaltum (or bitumen). An acid resistant component in etching grounds.

Binder. A substance such as gum, gelatin, rosin or drying oil, that "binds" or holds the pigment particles in an ink or paint.

Blanket. Rectangular woven wool felts placed between the roller of a press and the paper, used to transmit the pressure of the press during printing to the paper and plate.

Block-out (or stop-out). A varnish or hard ground liquid used to protect areas of an intaglio plate from acid.

Dutch Mordant. See Acid

Halftone Screen. A grid of dots or lines on plastic that produces the effect of continuous tone in a photo process. One can apply this screen to produce varied halftones on an intaglio plate.

Hard Ground. Substance made from rosin, beeswax and asphaltum, used to cover plates for etching. It can be applied as solid ball ground to a heated plate, or mixed with benzol or turpentine and brushed on as a liquid. Depending upon the desired quality of the etched line, the proportions vary. For fine lines the quantity of beeswax is increased; for deeper etching, asphaltum and rosin are increased.

India Stone. A man-made tool sharpening stone, excellent for sharpening burins and gouges. A round stone, with one coarse and one fine surface, is recommended.

Mordant. Acid used for biting plates. Specific mordants vary in chemical composition, strength and biting action.

Oil. Generally refers to drying oils, especially linseed, either cooked or raw, used in the preparation of printing inks.

Orthofilm. Film used by the graphic arts industry for photo transparencies. It produces a high contrast positive image and is used with dot screens for producing images with halftones.

Paper. In printmaking, refers to 100% rag, heavyweight paper (made from shredded cotton or linen rags). This paper is ideal for intaglio printmaking because of its high degree of flexibility.

Pigments. Finely-powdered substances used to color ink and paint. They are available as earth colors, chemical colors, and as colors from animal and vegetable source.

Plate. The metal support for an image in etching, engraving or lithography. Zinc and copper are the most commonly used metals for plates (zinc is easily etched in nitric acid; copper is etched in Dutch mordant or nitric acid or ferric chloride). Copper engraves beautifully and zinc is nicely suited to carving and gouging.

Polymer. A long molecule built up of many monomers (single unit molecules) linked together. ''Drying oils'' like linseed oil gradually thicken and polymerize on exposure to air, light and heat to form giant polymer chains. The understanding of the viscosity printmaking process is based on knowledge of the nature and behavior of polymers.

Printing Ink. Substance composed of pigment and binder (oil) used for the application of color. Printing inks are usually prepared by working cooked linseed oil into powdered pigment and grinding the mixture to a fine dispersion.

Resist. A surface varnish coating used to protect metal from corrosion by acid. Generally, resist is available as solid ball-ground or liquid hard ground.

Rollers. Cylinders constructed of various materials such as leather, rubber, gelatin and special plastics used to apply ink and grounds to various printmaking surfaces.

Rosin. A powdered resin made from pine sap, used to ground intaglio plates for aquatint. When melted onto the plate, rosin forms an extremely tough, resistant ground.

Soft Ground. A mixture of rosin, beeswax, asphaltum and grease. Soft ground is used for creating impressions of textures for etching (*see* Soft Ground Method).

Solvents. Various liquids such as turpentine, benzine, alcohol and kerosene, used to remove ink and ground from plates and from work areas.

Tarletan. Starched cotton gauze or muslin used to apply ink to the crevices of an intaglio plate or wipe ink from its surfaces.

Tools

Brayer. Small roller used to spread ink onto a plate or a woodblock.

Burin. An engraving tool that cuts lines in the plate.

Burnisher. A highly-polished, curved tool made of metal used to polish the plate, and to correct mistakes. The burnisher is kept polished by rubbing it on leather or chamois.

Damp Box. Closed box used to store damp paper prior to printing in order to maintain proper humidity.

Dust Box. An airtight box used to dust an etching plate with rosin powder for aquatint.

Echoppe. A dry point tool used to cut lines of varying width on the surface plate.

Gouge. A tool used to cut U-shaped crevices in a plate or woodblock.

Intaglio Press. The press used to print intaglio plates is composed of a steel bedplate which is lodged between upper and lower rollers. Usually the pressure of the upper roller is regulated by a set of calibrated screws. In intaglio printing the pressure must be strong enough to force the paper into the grooves of the plate with layers of felts, and so pull out the maximum amount of ink.

Rocker. A cutting implement whose serrated edge is used to produce a rough ink-holding surface on a mezzotint plate (*see* Mezzotint).

Rosin Bag. A small porous bag made of nylon, silk or cotton tissue used to dust the plate with rosin for aquatint.

Roulette. A tool for mezzotint having a textured, hardened-steel roller used to raise an ink-holding halftone.

Scorper. A flat engraving tool used to cut broad areas or lines on a plate.

Scraper. A triangular-bladed tool used to scrape and carve an intaglio plate or to remove unwanted areas in a plate. The scraper is frequently used to modify and grade the tonal structures produced by aquatint, mezzotint and deep bite.

Miscellaneous Terms

Acid Bath. A solution of acid and water.

Artist's Proof. Those prints, during the printing of an edition, reserved by the publisher for the artist.

Bevelling. The filing of the sharp edges of an intaglio plate to a slant; done to prevent the cutting of the paper and press felts during printing and especially to ensure that the press roller does not push the plate forward on the press bed.

Bleeding (or running). The tendency of an excessively oily ink to run or spread during the pressure of printing. Bleeding is especially common when an oily ink is used in the deeply bitten areas of an intaglio plate.

Burnishing. The process in which particular areas of the plate are polished so as to erase or smooth over marks made on it. Burnishing is commonly used in working aquatint and mezzotint areas of a plate to lighten their tone.

Chiaroscuro. Light to dark progression of tone.

Cross-hatching. A series of intersecting lines producing tonal variations in a print.

Edition Prints. A limited number of identical prints pulled from one or more original plates, stones or woodblocks, signed and numbered by the artist.

False-biting (or foul biting). Acid biting through a faultily laid coating of ground.

Feather Brushing. The use of a feather to brush away the bubbles that form on the intaglio plate while it sits in the acid bath.

Hand Wiping. Wiping the ink off the intaglio plate surface with the light, even pressure of the palm powdered with French chalk.

Hatching. A series of parallel lines producing tonal variations in a print.

Impression Number. The number of a print in an edition. It is usually expressed over the total number of prints in the edition.

Light Fastness. Ink's resistance to fading upon being exposed to light.

Light Sensitivity. A surface's tendency to change color upon being exposed to light.

Proof. A print used to check how the image has transferred from the plate to paper.

Pull. To transfer an image from an intaglio plate to paper.

Registration. The aligning of the plate or plates with the paper prior to transferring the image.

Steelfacing. Adding a layer of iron to the surface of an intaglio plate by electroplating. Steelfacing is generally used to insure the durability of the plate when printing large editions.

Tackiness. The binding quality or measure of stickiness of a solid or liquid. Tackiness is a physical property of printing inks; an understanding of it is essential in predicting the transfer of ink from plate to paper.

Viscosity. State of cohesiveness among molecules and polymer chains of a drying oil (such as cooked linseed oil) and its resultant resistance to flow. Sensitivity to the viscosity of inks is crucial to understanding how to modify them for printmaking, especially in the new methods of viscosity printmaking.

Wiping. The spreading of the proper amount of ink into the crevices of an intaglio plate and the removal of excess ink from its surface.

Select Bibliography

ADHEMAR, Jean. *The Caprices of Goya*. Paris: F. Hazan, 1951

———. *Twentieth Century Graphics*. New York: Praeger, 1971

ALBERS, Josef. *Interaction of Color*. New Haven: Yale University Press, 1975

American Craft Museum. *Making Paper*. New York: American Craft Council & International Paper Co., Carriage House Press, 1981

ANTREASIAN, Garo Z. & ADAMS, Clinton. *The Tamarind Book of Lithography: Art and Techniques*. New York: Harry N. Abrams Inc., 1971

APPS, E.A. *Ink Technology for Printers and Students,* Volume I. New York: Chemical Publishing Co., 1964

BANISTER, Manly. *Practical Guide to Etching*. New York: Dover Publications Inc., 1969

BARO, Gene. *Thirty Years of American Printmaking, Including the Twentieth National Print Exhibition*. New York: The Brooklyn Museum, 1976

BAUER, Max. *Precious Stones* Vol.I & II. New York: Dover Publications Inc., 1968

BAUGHMAN, Sara D., FIELD, Richard S., MANCOFF, Debra N., URBANELLI, Lora S., ZURIER, Rebecca. *American Prints 1900–1950*. New Haven: Yale University Art Gallery, 1983

BINYON, Laurence. *The Engraved Designs of William Blake*. New York: Da Capo Press, 1967

BIRREN, Faber. *Color*. Secaucus, N.J.: Citadel Press, 1963

———. *Functional Color*. New York: Crimson Press, 1937

———. *New Horizons in Color*. New York: Reinhold Publishing Co., 1955

———. *History of Color in Painting with New Principles of Color Expression*. New York: Reinhold Publishing Co., 1965

BLUM, Andre. *Les Origines du Papier, de l'Imprimerie et de la Gravure*. Paris: Editions de la Tournelle, 1935

Boston Museum of Fine Arts. *How to Care for Works of Art on Paper*. Boston: 1971

BOUMA, Pieter Johannes. *Physical Aspects of Color: An Introduction to the Scientific Study of Color Stimuli and Color Sensations*. Edited by de Groot, W., Kruithof, A.A., Ouweltjes, J.L. London: Macmillan Publishing Co., 1971

BRUNSDON, John. *The Technique of Etching & Engraving*. New York: Reinhold Publishing Co., 1965

BUCKLAND-WRIGHT, John. *Etching and Engraving: Techniques and the Modern Trend*. New York: The Studio Publications Inc., 1953

BURCH, R.M. *Colour Printing and Colour Printers*. London: Garland Publishing Inc., 1981

CARRINGTON, Fitzroy. *Prints and Their Makers: Essays on Engravers and Etchers, Old and Modern*. New York: Century Company, 1912

CASTLEMAN, Riva. *Printed Art: A View of Two Decades*. New York: Museum of Modern Art, 1980

CHAMBERLAIN, Walter. *Etching & Engraving*. London: Thames & Hudson, 1977

CHAMBERLIN, Gordon James. *Color, its Measurement, Computation and Application*. London & Philadelphia: Heyden Publishing, 1980

CHEVREUL, M.E. *The Principles of Harmony and Contrast of Colors and Their Applications to the Arts*. New York: Reinhold Publishing Co., 1967

COLLINS, Leo C. *Hercules Seghers*. Chicago: University of Chicago Press, 1953

EICHENBERG, Fritz. *The Art of the Print*. New York: Harry N. Abrams Inc., 1976

ESSICK, Robert N. *William Blake Printmaker*. New Jersey: Princeton University Press, 1980

EVANS, R.C. *An Introduction to Crystal Chemistry*. Cambridge: Cambridge University Press, 1939

FRIEDMAN, Joan M. *Color Printing in England 1486–1870*. New Haven: Yale Center for British Art, 1978

GALWEY, Andrew K. *Chemistry of Solids*. London: Chapman and Hall Ltd., 1967

GOLDMAN, Judith. *American Prints: Process and Proofs*. New York: Whitney Museum of American Art, Harper & Row, 1981

Graphic Work from the Bauhaus. Edited by Wingler, Hans N. Greenwich, Ct.: New York Graphics Society, 1969

GRAVES, Maitland. *Color Fundamentals*. New York: McGraw Hill Book Company Inc., 1952

HAYTER, S.W. *About Prints*. London: Oxford University Press, 1962

———. *New Ways of Gravure, Revised Edition*. New York: Watson-Guptil Publications, 1981

HELLER, Jules. *Printmaking Today*. New York: Henry Holt and Company Inc., 1958

———. *Papermaking*. New York: Watson-Guptil Publications, 1982

HELLMAN, Harold. *The Art and Science of Color*. New York: McGraw Hill, 1967

HERBERTS, Kurt. *The Complete Book of Artists' Techniques*. New York: Praeger, 1958

HIND, Arthur M. *A History of Engraving & Etching*. New York: Dover Publications Inc., 1963

HUGHES, Sukey. *Washi: The World of Japanese Paper*. Tokyo: Kodansha International, 1978

HUGO, Ian. *New Eyes on the Art of Engraving*. New York: "Outcast" Series of Chapbooks, No.7, Oscar Baradinsky, Alicat Bookshop, 1946

ITTEN, Johannes. *The Art of Color*. New York. Van Nostrand Reinhold Co., 1973

IVINS, William Mills. *Prints and Visual Communication*. New York: Da Capo Press, 1969

JOHNSON, Una E. *American Prints and Printmakers*. New York: Doubleday & Co., 1980

KANDINSKY, W. *Concerning the Spiritual in Art*. New York: Wittenborn, Schultz, 1947

KEPES, Gyorgy, Ed., *The Language of Vision*. Chicago: Theobald, 1944

KLEE, Paul. *The Thinking Eye*. London: Percy Lund, Humphries & Co. Ltd., 1961

KONHEIM, Linda (introduction). *Prints from the Guggenheim Museum Collection*. New York: Solomon R. Guggenheim Foundation, 1978

KORETSKY, Elaine & TOALE, Bernard (Directors). *International Conference of Hand Papermakers*. New York: Carriage House Press, 1981

KUEPPERS, Harald. *The Basic Law of Color Theory*. New York: Barron's, 1982

LABARRE, E.J. *Dictionary & Encyclopedia of Paper & Papermaking*. Amsterdam: Swets & Zeltlingen, 1952

LAPP, Ralph E. and Editors of Time-Life Books. *Matter*. New York: Time-Life Books, 1969

LARSEN, Louis M. *Industrial Printing Inks*. New York: Reinhold Publishing Co., 1962

LE BLON, J.C. *Coloritto*. New York: Van Nostrand Reinhold Co., 1980

LISTER, Raymond. *Prints and Printmaking*. London: Metheun London Ltd., 1984

MARGERISON, D. & EAST, G.C. *An Introduction to Polymer Chemistry*. Oxford: Pergamon Press, 1967

MARK, Herman and Editors of Time-Life Books. *Giant Molecules*. New York: Time-Life Books, 1968

MAYER, Ralph. *The Artists Handbook of Materials & Techniques*. New York: Viking Press, 1982

MAYOR, Alpheus Hyatt. *Popular Prints of the Americas*. New York: Crown Publishers, 1973

MOSER, Joann. *Atelier 17*. Madison: University of Wisconsin, 1977

MUELLER, Conrad G., RUDOLPH, Mae and Editors of Time-Life Books. *Light and Vision*. New York: Time-Life Books, 1969

NAPIM (National Association of Printing Ink Manufacturers) *Printing Ink Handbook*.

NASSAU, Kurt. *The Physics and Chemistry of Color: The Fifteen Causes of Color*. New York: Wiley, 1983

NEWMAN, Thelma R. *Innovative Printmaking*. New York: Crown Publishers, 1977

New York Graphic Society. *Rembrandt: Experimental Etcher*. (catalogue). Greenwich, Ct.: N.Y.G.A., 1969

OSBORNE, Roy. *Lights and Pigments: Color Principle for Artists*. New York: Harper & Row, 1980

PERNI, Andy. *New Color Guide*. New York: The Perni Color Process Corp., 1986

PETERDI, Gabor. *Printmaking*. New York: Macmillan Publishing Co. Inc., 1971

PRICE, Charles C. *Geometry of Molecules*. New York: McGraw Hill Inc., 1971

REDDY, N. Krishna. "Some Notes on Recent Methods of Simultaneous Structuring of Intaglio and Surface Colors in Printmaking," *Krishna Reddy: A Retrospective*. New York: Bronx Museum of the Arts, 1981

REESE, Albert. *American Prize Prints of the Twentieth Century*. New York: American Artists Group, 1949

ROSS, John & ROMANO, Clare. *The Complete Printmaker*. New York: Free Press, 1972

SAFF, Donald & SACILOTTO, Deli. *The History and Process of Printmaking*. New York: Holt, Rinehart and Winston, 1978

SALTMAN, David. *Paper Basics: forestry, manufacture, selection purchasing, mathematics, metrics, recycling*. New York: Van Nostrand Reinhold Co., 1978

SARGENT, Walter. *The Enjoyment and Use of Color:* Toronto: General Publishing Company Ltd., 1964

SEYMOUR, Raymond B. *Introduction to Polymer Chemistry*. New York: McGraw Hill Inc., 1971

STERNBERG, Harry. *Modern Methods & Materials of Etching*. New York: McGraw Hill Inc., 1949

STUDLEY, Vance. *The Art and Craft of Hand Papermaking*. New York: Van Nostrand Reinhold, 1977

THOMAS, Ann Wall. *Colors from the Earth*. New York: Van Nostrand Reinhold, 1980

THOMPSON, Daniel. *The Materials and Techniques of Medieval Painting*. New York: Dover Publications Inc., 1956

TOCH, Maximillian. *The Chemistry and Technology of Mixed Paints*. New York: Van Nostrand Reinhold, 1907

TREVELYAN, Julian. *Etching: Modern Methods of Intaglio Printmaking*. New York: Watson-Guptil Publications Inc., 1964

VAN LEUSDEN, Willem. *The Etchings of Hercules Seghers*. Utrecht: A.W. Bruna and Zonn, 1961

WENNIGER, Mary Ann. *Collagraph Printmaking*. New York: Watson-Guptil, 1975

WILLIAMS, Robert. *The Geometrical Foundation of Natural Structure*. New York: Dover Publications Inc., 1979

WILLIAMSON, Samuel J. *Light and Color in Nature and Art*. New York: Wiley, 1983

WOOD, Elizabeth A. *Crystals & Light*. New York: Dover Publications Inc., 1977

World Print Council (Ed. Paulette Long). *Paper, Art and Technology*. New York: The World Print Council, 1979

Yale Art Gallery Associates. *Color in Prints*. New Haven: Yale University Art Gallery Bulletin, Vol.27, No.3, Vol.28, No.1, October 1962

ZIGROSSER, Carl. *The Artist in America: Contemporary Printmakers*. New York: Hacker Art Books, 1978

Index